AF606927

IMAGES
of America

Oak Hill Cemetery

Oak Hill Cemetery is so much more than the final resting place of tens of thousands of Washingtonians. Oak Hill's peaceful garden is the perfect playground for city wildlife, including chipmunks, squirrels, rabbits, foxes, deer, and many different types of birds. Following a funeral service, no floral tribute left behind is safe from the hungry deer that make themselves at home once the gates close to visitors at 4:30 p.m. (Courtesy of the author.)

On the Cover: Located on a hillside descending to Rock Creek in Washington DC, Oak Hill Cemetery is simply stunning in every season. The winter view of Oak Hill is the most unobstructed, with clear views of historic memorials that cannot be found from the same vantage point while in summer's full bloom. The Corcoran Mausoleum, centered, is the final resting place of Oak Hill's founder, William Wilson Corcoran. (Courtesy of Library of Congress.)

IMAGES
of America

OAK HILL CEMETERY

Laura Lavelle (née Hackfeld)

Copyright © 2024 by Laura Lavelle (née Hackfeld)
ISBN 978-1-4671-6088-9

Published by Arcadia Publishing
Charleston, South Carolina

Printed in the United States of America

Library of Congress Control Number: Applied for

For all general information, please contact Arcadia Publishing:
Telephone 843-853-2070
Fax 843-853-0044
E-mail sales@arcadiapublishing.com

Visit us on the Internet at www.arcadiapublishing.com

Dedicated to the ghostly friends I have made while writing, and to my late honey husband, Michael James Lavelle. Our love will never die.

Contents

ACKNOWLEDGMENTS

I wish to acknowledge the loving community of family and friends who made this book possible through their encouragement and support. First and foremost, a million thanks to the lovely Ella Pozell, who graciously offered herself to the book's introduction and shared her wealth of knowledge: I am forever grateful. To Paul Williams, my mentor and friend, without whom this book would not exist: thank you for volunteering me to write this! To Lou Krach, who introduced me to Oak Hill Cemetery, and Dave Jackson, the superintendent who hired me and encouraged me to learn: you started it all. To friends Greg Alexander, Shantel Lester, and Evan Washington and cemetery board members David de Vicq and George Hill, thank you for supporting me through this long and tedious process. To my family: David, Greta, Nathan, Fen, and Zachary (Hackfelds), and Robert and Sharon Lavelle: I would not be where I am today without you all standing with me. Last but never least, to Michael James Lavelle, I am forever grateful for the life and love we shared in our time together. I will always love you.

On the research side of things, I would like thank Robert LaRose from the DC Public Library; Haley Wilkinson from Tudor Place Historic House and Garden, Washington DC; Marisa Bourgoin from the Archives of American Art; Christopher Anglim and Phomika Murray from the University of the District of Columbia; Michelle Krawl from the Library of Congress, and Jerry Frishman for their generosity with sharing photographs.

Photographs for this book taken by the author will be credited as (LL). All other image sources have been credited as follows: Archive of American Art (AAA); DC Public Library, People's Archive (DCPL-PA); Jefferson College Historical Society (JCHS); Jerry Frishman; the Library of Congress (LOC); Massachusetts Historical Society (MHS); the Mount Vernon Ladies' Association; Oak Hill Cemetery (OHC); Smithsonian Institution Archives (SIA); Tudor Place Historic House and Garden, Washington DC; the University Archives of the University of the District of Columbia; and Willem van de Poll, Nationaal Archief/Van de Poll.

INTRODUCTION

In the 1830s, the Romantic Cemetery Movement began in the United States (having already begun in Europe) with the establishment of Mount Auburn Cemetery in Cambridge, Massachusetts. These rural-style garden cemeteries became de facto parks because of their plantings of lovely flowers and shrubs, winding pathways with "weeping" species of trees, towering oaks, and sweeping vistas. Wealthy merchant William Wilson Corcoran felt a strong desire to create such a cemetery in his hometown of Georgetown and found that Parrott's Woods, a 15-acre tract of forested land descending to Rock Creek, certainly displayed all of the attributes of a future garden cemetery. Corcoran purchased the land in 1848 from George Corbin Washington (a great-nephew of the first president) and his son Lewis W. Washington, and on March 3, 1849, the 30th Congress passed an act to incorporate Oak Hill Cemetery in the District of Columbia. During the Civil War, Corcoran purchased an additional 10 acres from the Davidson family, whose property abutted the cemetery's east side. The only stipulation was that the Davidson family would have a burial lot, and it is shown on the cemetery map as Davidson Circle.

The first cemetery lots were sold at public auction on October 17, 1851, after master engineer George de la Roche had supervised the grading and layout of burial spaces. Most of the early lots contained 300 square feet and were priced at 40¢ per foot. Corcoran chose Lots 1–15 for himself and erected a beautiful mausoleum designed by Thomas U. Walter, the architect of the US Capitol. The names inscribed at the top of the structure are "Corcoran" and "Eustis" (his daughter having married George Eustis Jr.). James Renwick was chosen by Corcoran to design the nondenominational chapel on the ellipse. Other notable Renwick designs include the Smithsonian Castle and St. Patrick's Cathedral in New York City.

It is a harsh reality that a mid-19th-century cemetery would contain the remains of thousands of children. Oak Hill is no exception. The first burial at the cemetery was Eleanor Ann Washington, age 26, who was interred on April 13, 1849, a month after the cemetery's founding. She was the daughter of George C. and Ann T. Washington, from whom Corcoran purchased the cemetery land. Dr. Charles White and his wife, Mary, buried five children in their Lot 295 East: Mary Eliza, age 12; Winifred Emily, age 10; Charles Clarence, age 9; and Louise Madeline, age 4, all of whom died of scarlet fever, and a stillborn child who died on July 11, 1880. The inscription at the bottom of their monument reads: "Thy Will Be Done."

The most notable child interment was that of William "Willie" Wallace Lincoln, son of Pres. Abraham Lincoln, who died on February 20, 1862, and was temporarily placed in the Carroll Mausoleum with the thought that he would be removed at the end of Lincoln's second term. Tragically, Lincoln was assassinated just 42 days into his second presidential term, and Willie's casket was removed on April 21, 1865, to join his father by train back to their home state of Illinois. Willie's story was reborn by author George Saunders in his award-winning 2017 novel *Lincoln in the Bardo*, exploring the president's grief and Willie's soul learning to navigate the *bardo*, the space between death and the afterlife. The story takes place at Oak Hill Cemetery, and fans of the novel still flock to the Carroll Mausoleum daily to follow in the footsteps of President Lincoln.

Through the 175 years of Oak Hill's existence, the four-member board of managers, superintendents, and groundskeepers have endeavored to perpetuate two of Corcoran's visions: to "awe the visitor" upon entering the grounds and to run the cemetery as a nonprofit entity, which it remains to this day. Because of Oak Hill's unique location—Rock Creek on the north and east, Thirtieth Street on the south, and Montrose Park on the west—the cemetery had no means to expand and meet the needs of those wanting to buy space in this historic and beautiful place. Therefore, in 1984, the board of managers embarked upon an innovative program to use Oak Hill's ample walkways and steps as burial spaces.

The first project was that of replacing steps below the Corcoran Mausoleum, yielding 20 cremation sites. Although a bit unconventional, the steps were well received, and as the years passed, more were reclaimed so that now there are close to 400. David Jackson, superintendent from 2012 to 2021, had the idea of placing boxes beside existing steps to further add to inventory. He also found more crumbling pathways and replaced them with casket and cremation sites.

In 1986, the Reno Hill area was chosen for a pathway crypt project. The deteriorating pathways were removed, and 40 double-casket crypts were placed therein. Thirty-six cremation vaults holding up to 10 urns were also installed. Since those early years, replacement of steps and pathways has continued to include the pathway around the Renwick Chapel, which now contains 96 in-ground cremation sites. In 2011, the Willow Columbarium was constructed beside Rock Creek and contains 420 cremation niches. New mausoleums are now a part of the ellipse and serve as lovely additions to the cemetery's entrance.

For 28 years, former superintendent Ella Pozell considered herself privileged to meet and work with families in their greatest hour of need. Ella and her late husband, Joe, began working at Oak Hill Cemetery and living in the beautiful Gatehouse in 1984. Their son Joseph was five years old at the time and found that the house and grounds had ample space for friends and dogs. Joe became superintendent in 1985 and died in 2005, and Ella stepped into the superintendent role until her retirement in 2012. Joe is interred in Honeysuckle Pathway, which will also be Ella's permanent residence someday.

Neither Joe nor Ella ever dreaded a day at work, because they knew that they would perhaps learn interesting information about the cemetery's history through family contacts or their own research, both often resulting in fascinating stories. After every interment, Joe and Ella would walk to the site and have a moment with Oak Hill's newest permanent resident.

In the years following her retirement, Ella's thoughts often return to Oak Hill. Ella has been invited back to Oak Hill every year since her departure, graciously working in the office while her successive superintendents vacation. During her visits, the names she sees on memorial stones fondly remind her of the bonds forged with families and how they became part of her and Joe's family. She feels confident that the future of Oak Hill is secure and is honored to have been given the opportunity to share her story in the introduction of what she knows will be a fascinating book.

One

Oak Hill's Deep Roots

The beautiful grounds of the first rural-style garden cemetery in Washington DC used to be called Parrott's Woods, a wooded, wild retreat and gathering ground for Georgetown's early residents. Once a place for Fourth of July picnics, ropewalks, and political protests, Parrott's Woods was transformed into a sacred burial ground when an act of Congress established the Oak Hill Cemetery on March 3, 1849. (Courtesy of OHC.)

William Wilson Corcoran was born in Georgetown in 1798 and made his wealth as a cofounder of Riggs Bank (now PNC), which financed the federal government during the Mexican-American War. Corcoran also loved art and amassed a large collection of American art that he displayed in an institution of his own creation: the Corcoran Gallery of Art. The original home of the Corcoran Gallery, on the northeast corner of Pennsylvania Avenue and Seventeenth Street, now houses the Smithsonian Institution's Renwick Gallery, and the artwork residing within was disbursed across countless organizations in the DC area. In 1848, Corcoran purchased 12 acres of land from George Corbin Washington, a grand nephew of George Washington, with the intention of building a cemetery for the neighborhood of Georgetown. He was a Confederate sympathizer and generous philanthropist who maintained an active role as president of the cemetery board throughout the rest of his life. (Courtesy of LOC.)

Oak Hill was not the first cemetery in Georgetown when Corcoran purchased the land in 1848. The historically black Mount Zion and Female Union Band Society (FUBS) cemeteries, Oak Hill's easterly neighbors, began burials in 1808. Upon Oak Hill's opening in 1849, several families buried within the Mount Zion and FUBS cemeteries were removed and reburied in Oak Hill, which was only available to rich white citizens. (Courtesy of LOC.)

The first person buried at Oak Hill was a young woman named Eleanor Ann Washington. Eleanor was the only daughter of George Corbin Washington and was known for her kindness and intelligence. Having grown up on this land, Eleanor was afforded the opportunity to choose her own burial site in Lot 50 prior to her death at the age of 26. (Courtesy of LL.)

In the late 1790s, the future Capt. George de la Roche was sold into indentured servitude to a maritime captain, apprenticing a rough life upon the sea. Upon turning 21, de la Roche bought his freedom and joined the US Navy for the War of 1812. Following his service, de la Roche returned to the sea on merchant ships and faced pirates in the Caribbean. When he was ready to leave sea life behind, de la Roche pursued a career in engineering and architecture. Captain de la Roche had already designed Washington DC's Old Naval Observatory when Corcoran asked him to survey and lay out the terraced hills of Oak Hill. Captain de la Roche's attention to detail and his drainage designs have ensured Oak Hill's continuing life and legacy. The captain now rests forever in Lot 306. (Both, courtesy of LL.)

The Gatehouse at Oak Hill was built in the 1850s to house the cemetery's superintendent and family and is believed to have been designed by Capt. George de la Roche. It was originally built in a Gothic style and has been added to and renovated many times to accommodate growing staff families. The renovation to add the bell tower added a third floor and changed the style of the house from Gothic to Italianate. The Gatehouse also houses the cemetery company's office and is attached to the cemetery's Bigelow Iron Fence, which is currently undergoing an intensive multimillion-dollar restoration. (Both, courtesy of LOC.)

Oak Hill Cemetery's chapel was among the first structures built on the cemetery grounds. W.W. Corcoran commissioned James Renwick Jr. to construct the Gothic Revival–style, one-room chapel at the crest of Oak Hill. The cornerstone was laid in 1850, and construction took three years to complete. The body of the Renwick Chapel was built with Potomac blue gneiss, and the roof was tiled with purple slate from Vermont. Red sandstone from the Seneca quarry in Maryland was used as caps for the exterior buttresses, as well as for the framing of the door and windows. It was Renwick's masterful use of this same Seneca sandstone for the Smithsonian Institution's Castle in 1846 that led to the commission of Oak Hill's miniature Gothic gem. (Above, courtesy of DCPL-PA; below, courtesy of LOC.)

Two converted gas lamps bring light inside the Renwick Chapel, illuminating an ornately carved oak wall trim and ceiling embellished with medallions that match with a pair of carved oak chairs abutting the altar. Twelve pews line the central aisle, which is also lined by four vaults under the floor that were built for temporary casket storage, most recently used in 2016. Crown molding caps 10 stained-glass windows, with the rear rose window completely encircled with the decorative trim. Many funeral and memorial services have taken place in the chapel, as well as book club and cemetery board meetings, baptisms, and intimate weddings. (Both, courtesy of LOC.)

Stephen Bloomer Balch was the founding pastor of the Bridge Street Presbyterian Church in Georgetown, now called the Georgetown Presbyterian Church. Balch was also a Revolutionary War veteran and an educator, and during the War of 1812, Balch led a group of students to battle in Maryland. Balch is buried in Lot 686, which includes a large monument placed in his honor. (Courtesy of LL.)

Uriah Forrest was a Revolutionary War veteran and amputee, having lost a leg at the Battle of Germantown. He went on to become a delegate for the State of Maryland, a representative to the Continental Congress, and the third mayor of Georgetown from 1792 to 1793. His house on M Street in Georgetown now serves as the Ukrainian Embassy, and he is buried in Lot 255 East. (Courtesy of LL.)

Edward Linthicum was the founder of a hardware store in Georgetown and started the Linthicum Institute to teach young white boys. Perhaps Linthicum's most lasting legacy is as a one-time owner of Dumbarton Oaks, a large estate and garden that is currently owned and managed by Harvard University. The Linthicum Mausoleum in Lot 242 is a striking red sandstone miniature chapel, pictured here in the 1850s. (Courtesy of OHC.)

John Adlum was a veteran of both the Revolutionary War and the War of 1812 and a pioneer in American viticulture. From his farm in Maryland, Adlum cultivated the Catawba grape and corresponded with Thomas Jefferson on best wine practices, publishing America's first book on the culture of winemaking. Originally buried elsewhere, the remains of Adlum and his wife were reburied in Oak Hill Lot 133 in 1864. (Courtesy of LL.)

On February 28, 1844, aboard the USS *Princeton*, a new cannon developed by Capt. Robert Stockton called the Peacemaker exploded during a demonstration cruise for government and military guests along the Potomac River. Pres. John Tyler was below deck with former first lady Dolley Madison when the explosion occurred on the main deck of the ship. Six people died because of this insufficiently tested weapon, including Secretary of State Abel Parker Upshur and Capt. Beverly Kennon, the chief of the Bureau of Construction, Equipment, and Repairs. All victims were originally buried at Congressional Cemetery in Southeast DC, and Captain Kennon and Upshur were moved to Oak Hill Cemetery in 1874. (Both, courtesy of LL.)

Following the tragic and unexpected death of Captain Kennon aboard the USS *Princeton*, his widow, Britannia, and their four-month-old daughter, Markie, returned to live at her family home in Georgetown called Tudor Place. Britannia was born at Tudor Place in 1815 to the estate's original owners, Thomas Peter and Mary Parke Custis, a granddaughter of Martha Washington. Britannia grew up at Tudor Place and married Captain Kennon in the drawing room there in 1842. Following the death of her mother in 1854, Britannia inherited the estate and took responsibility for the care and management of the property and the family. She remained there as reigning matriarch for the rest of her life, outliving her daughter and son-in-law. Britannia died at home on the night before her 96th birthday, splitting the house between her five grandchildren. Britannia is buried with her husband in Oak Hill Lot 544. (Courtesy of LOC.)

Baron Alexander de Bodisco's official title was "chamberlain private counselor of his majesty the emperor of all the Russias, his envoy extraordinary and minister plenipotentiary," and he served as Russia's first ambassador to the United States from 1838 to 1854. In 1840, at the age of 54, de Bodisco married 16-year-old Harriet Beall Williams in an extravagant ceremony at his residence at 3322 O Street in Georgetown. While the high-society affair attracted famous guests such as Henry Clay, James Buchanan, and then-president Martin van Buren, local citizens rudely referred to the couple as "Beauty and the Beast." The couple made a happy home together for 14 years, and Harriet remarried after de Bodisco passed away in 1854. The angel topping his impressive monument in Lot 396.5 now faces east, toward Russia. (Left, courtesy of LOC; below, courtesy of DCPL-PA.)

Jacob Fussell was a Quaker abolitionist and dairy man who was the first to make ice cream commercially available in the United States. In 1851, Fussell began using excess cream from his dairy delivery to make ice cream and shipped it by train from his facility in Pennsylvania. He expanded to open ice cream factories in DC and Baltimore as well as shops in Boston and New York City. Fussell's frozen treats were widely available around the DC area, including at early Washington Nationals baseball games at the turn of the 20th century. Fussell, known as the "Father of Ice Cream Industry," was also a fervent Quaker abolitionist who operated a stop on the Underground Railroad. Fussell rests in Oak Hill Lot 149 East. (Above, courtesy of LOC; below, courtesy of LL.)

Marcia Burnes Van Ness was known during her lifetime as "The Heiress of Washington." Her father, David Burnes, was well known to early government officials, as his 600-acre farm sat in the middle of where officials wanted to build the federal campus. Burnes had famously rejected an offer from George Washington but slowly started selling off pieces of his farm to the government in the 1790s. Refusing to give up his life and livelihood on the tobacco farm that had been passed down by his family since the 1690s, Burnes and his family continued to live in this little cottage amid the construction of the federal city. Marcia was the sole heiress to her father's fortune when he passed away in 1799, as her brother had already passed away. (Above, courtesy of LOC; left, courtesy of OHC.)

Marcia Burnes married John Peter Van Ness, a congressman from New York, in 1802, and the couple lived in the Burnes cottage until a mansion designed for them on Seventeenth Street by Benjamin Henry Latrobe was completed in 1816. Marcia retired from the social obligations of high society following the death of her daughter and granddaughter from childbirth in 1823 and threw herself into charitable pursuits. Marcia was the financial benefactor and eventual director of the Washington City Orphan Asylum and held that position until her death in 1832. Congress adjourned early for her funeral, the first time in American history that this honor was bestowed to a woman. Designed by George Hadfield in 1833 and inspired by the Roman Temple of Vesta, the Van Ness Mausoleum was moved to Oak Hill Cemetery between late 1872 and early 1873 and was placed on the National Register of Historic Places in 1982. (Courtesy of DCPL-PA.)

Myrtilla Miner was the fifth of six children born to a deacon in New York in 1815 and grew up with the desire to become an educator. In 1846, Myrtilla moved south to Mississippi to teach at a school for the daughters of wealthy plantation owners. Once there, Myrtilla witnessed for the first time the horrible cruelty of plantation owners to the enslaved adults and children, and was forced to leave her position after asking to teach the enslaved girls who were excluded. Myrtilla moved back north with a clear mission from God in mind: create a school to teach African American girls to become teachers themselves. In 1854, Myrtilla opened the Normal School for Colored Girls in Washington DC, teaching her students a wide range of subjects including math, science, and personal hygiene. (Courtesy of the University Archives of the University of the District of Columbia.)

Faced with violent threats from racists that forced the school to relocate three times within its first few years, Myrtilla learned to handle a firearm for protection and never faltered in her mission to teach. She fundraised for her school across the country, making friends with abolitionists like Frederick Douglass and Harriet Beecher Stowe. Myrtilla Miner tragically passed away after complications from a carriage accident in 1864 at the age of 49 and is buried in Oak Hill Lot 439 East. Her school was renamed Miner Normal School in 1879, and in 1929, the school was renamed once again to Miner Teacher's College. The college combined with Wilson Teacher's College in 1955, and the name evolved to the University of the District of Columbia. Miner Elementary School in DC is named in her honor. (Courtesy of the University Archives of the University of the District of Columbia.)

Nancy M. Johnson (left) was an educator, abolitionist, mother, and inventor. She married Walter R. Johnson in 1823, and together they adopted a son and a daughter. In 1843, Nancy M. Johnson successfully submitted a patent for the first hand-cranked ice cream maker, making ice cream accessible to those who did not own an icebox. Her design is still widely used today! Nancy was also a close friend to Myrtilla Miner and became one of the incorporators of Miner's school. She further served on the school's board of directors to help the school after Miner's death in 1864. Nancy, alongside her sister Mary Ann Donaldson (below), traveled to South Carolina as missionaries to teach formerly enslaved people from 1862 to 1865. The sisters later returned to Washington DC, and the entire family is buried in Oak Hill Lot 54. (Both, courtesy of LOC.)

Walter W. Johnson was the adopted son of Nancy M. Johnson and Walter R. Johnson, the first secretary of the American Association for the Advancement of Science. Walter W. was an abolitionist and educator and spent time as a guest lecturer of astronomy at the Miner School. Walter tragically passed away in a mine shaft accident in 1879 and is buried with his family in Oak Hill Lot 54. (Courtesy of LOC.)

Richard Cutts served as a comptroller of the US Treasury as well as a House representative for Massachusetts from 1801 to 1813. Cutts married the sister of Dolley Madison, and his daughter cultivated a close relationship with her aunt. Dolley lived with the Cutts family in this house on Lafayette Square for the last 12 years of her life. The Cutts family burial site is located in Lot 407. (Courtesy of LOC.)

The private estate of Evermay has served as Oak Hill Cemetery's eastern border since the cemetery's founding in 1849. The mansion and grounds were owned by the Davidson family, who earned their wealth through real estate dealings with the federal government and sold the land that the White House was later built upon. It was with the profits from the White House sale that the Davidson family commissioned British architect Nicholas King to construct Evermay in 1802. In the 1860s, the Davidsons sold 10 acres of their property abutting Oak Hill to the cemetery and were granted the honor of a large family site called the Davidson Circle. Today, Evermay is owned by Japanese businesswoman Sachiko Kuno and serves as the home for her charitable organization, S&R Evermay, cofounded with her ex-husband, Ryugi Ueno. One of the functions of the organization is supporting the Evermay Visionaries, providing scholarships and work space for five women a year at the Evermay estate. (Courtesy of LOC.)

Two

THE CIVIL WAR

When the Civil War broke out between the Union and the Confederacy in 1861, the Potomac River separating Maryland and DC from Virginia served as the region's Mason-Dixon Line. Oak Hill Cemetery is the final resting place for numerous military officers from both sides of the battle. Buried here in sacred rest, soldiers of the Blue and Gray are equal in death. (Courtesy of OHC.)

Capt. Alois Babo (left) and 1st Lt. Reinhold Wesselhoeft (below) were both German-born immigrants from the Boston area who volunteered to serve with the Union army. Working together, they were successful in creating a volunteer company comprised of German-born immigrants. Their company mustered into service with the 20th Regiment of Massachusetts Volunteers in July 1861 and traveled by train to DC before marching to Poolesville, Maryland, to support the Union border along the Potomac River across from Leesburg, Virginia. On the eve of October 21, 1861, Union scouts wrongly reported an abandoned Confederate camp, atop Ball's Bluff. Union general Charles Stone, working with bad intel, began ferrying Union troops across the Potomac with orders to ascend Ball's Bluff and claim Confederate territory. (Both, courtesy of MHS.)

The Battle of Ball's Bluff began in the early-morning hours of October 21, 1861, when Confederate troops realized that Union forces had crossed to the Virginia side of the Potomac River. The first shots were fired around dawn, and the battle lasted most of the day, with the 20th Massachusetts playing a central role in the Union defense. When his commanding officer fell to an injury, Lieutenant Wesselhoeft took control of Company C amidst the chaos of battle. As the skirmish came to a close and Union forces began their retreat, Captain Babo and Lieutenant Wesselhoeft were seen swimming together across the Potomac River while under heavy Confederate gunfire. One of them was heard crying out in German that they had been shot before they both disappeared in the water. Wesselhoeft's body was found two weeks after the battle 15 miles downriver from Ball's Bluff, while Babo's body was never recovered. Babo is honored on Wesselhoeft's headstone, found in Oak Hill Lot 491A No. 33. (Courtesy of LL.)

William Orton Williams (right, seated) and Walter Gibson "Gip" Peter (left, standing) were cousins who were both raised locally in the Washington area and joined the Confederacy at the outbreak of the war. Peter served as an aide de camp during the Battle of Ball's Bluff. While their motives have never been made known, Williams and Peter snuck into a Union camp in Tennessee on June 8, 1863, impersonating Union officers. The pair were quickly discovered and apprehended as spies and were hanged the next morning. Their relatives at Tudor Place in Georgetown paid to have their bodies returned to DC in 1864, and they were reburied in Oak Hill Lot 578. (Left, courtesy of Tudor Place Historic House and Garden, Washington DC; below, courtesy of LL.)

Gen. Jesse Reno is one of the most recognizable Civil War officers today, known as the namesake of Reno, Nevada, and DC's Fort Reno. General Reno was a decorated Army officer who had graduated from West Point in 1846 and demonstrated his military prowess during the Mexican-American War. When the Civil War started, he was appointed brigadier general, leading troops through victories in North Carolina and Virginia before he was tragically killed by a misfire within his own troops at the Battle of South Mountain in western Maryland. Reno's body was held in Boston until his wife arranged for his burial within a newly opened section of Oak Hill Cemetery now called Reno Hill. In addition to his striking crepe-draped column memorial in Oak Hill Lot 686, a large monument stands in his honor at the South Mountain Battlefield Park. (Courtesy of LL.)

Col. Henry W. Kingsbury was born into a military family, and following the death of his father, he was taken underwing by famous Union general Ambrose Burnside. He graduated from West Point in 1861 and shortly after married the niece of Pres. Zachary Taylor. Kingsbury took command of the 11th Connecticut Volunteer Infantry at the age of 25, leading a fatal charge against Confederate forces at Burnside Bridge at the Battle of Antietam on September 17, 1862. His brother-in-law Gen. David R. Jones led the Confederate division that caused his death. Kingsbury never met his son, who was born just weeks following his father's tragic death. Both Colonel Kingsbury and his son are buried in Oak Hill Lot 640. (Above, courtesy of LOC; below, courtesy of LL.)

Samuel Powhatan Carter was the only soldier in American history to hold official commissions in both the US Army and Navy. Carter enlisted with the US Navy in 1840, serving as a midshipman for five years before enrolling at the US Naval Academy. Following his graduation in 1846, Carter saw action in the Mexican-American War and taught at the Naval Academy prior to the Civil War. Carter was asked to support the Union, and he was mustered into the US Army as a brigadier general in 1862. He led infantry brigades through Kentucky, Tennessee, and North Carolina, returning to the US Navy after the Civil War. Carter retired in 1881 with the rank of rear admiral. Carter is buried in Oak Hill Lot 822. (Right, courtesy of LOC; below, courtesy of LL.)

Antonia Ford was living with her family in Fairfax Courthouse, Virginia, when the Civil War started in 1861, and the Fords were forced to quarter Union soldiers in their home, which still stands today in Fairfax, Virginia. Antonia used her unique position to collect military intel and gossip and was made an honorary aide de camp by Confederate general J.E.B. Stuart in 1861. She was suspected of assisting Confederate colonel John Mosby with the midnight raid of Fairfax Courthouse and capture of Union general Edwin Stoughton. Mosby denied her involvement. Antonia was ultimately arrested for espionage in 1863 and was escorted to the Old Capitol Prison by Union major Joseph C. Willard, one of the soldiers who had been boarded in her family's home and cofounder of DC's Willard Hotel. (Right, courtesy of LOC; below, courtesy of LL.)

During her prison sentence, Antonia and Major Willard kept a written correspondence and ultimately fell in love. Willard helped Antonia achieve her freedom: he supervised Antonia as she swore her loyalty to the Union, and she was released. The happy couple were married in 1864 but faced many hardships together. Antonia faced health issues that stemmed from her time in the Old Capitol Prison, and the Willards endured the loss of three young children. Antonia passed away at 32 years old in 1871, leaving Joseph a widower and a single father for the rest of his life. Willard's papers at the Library of Congress indicate that Joseph continued to think of and honor Antonia until his death in 1897. Joseph and Antonia forever rest together in Oak Hill's Lot 689. (Right, courtesy of LOC; below, courtesy of LL.)

Gen. Seth Eastman made his career in the US Army as a teacher, mapmaker, and illustrator. Eastman was a multitalented artist who painted landscapes of US Army forts as well as sketches of Native American life and traditions of the Western territories with fine detail. Eastman graduated from West Point in 1829 and had already been stationed at Fort Snelling in Minnesota twice by 1835. Eastman and his second wife, Mary Henderson Eastman, took great interest in studying the customs and traditions of Native American tribes near the fort. Eastman's painted scenes of Native American life were used as illustrations for a Congressional study of Native American culture. Several of his landscapes still hang in the US Capitol. Eastman and his wife are buried in Oak Hill Lot 652. (Left, courtesy of LOC; below, courtesy of LL.)

Gen. William Birney was an American soldier, abolitionist, educator, and lawyer who is notably remembered for enlisting thousands of free black men in the US Army. Birney and his wife, Catherine, were married in 1846 and moved to France, where Birney taught English for two years at a Bourges university. The couple returned to the United States in 1853, and Birney practiced law until the Civil War. Birney organized and led at least seven regiments of freed black troops through the South and participated in the Appomattox campaign, which led to Lee's surrender. Following the war, he returned to his private law practice in Washington DC and served as DC's attorney general before passing away in 1907. Birney and his wife are buried with their family in Oak Hill Lot 67 East. (Both, courtesy of LOC.)

Albert Pike served as a brigadier general in the Confederate army for one year before he was forced to resign due to disagreements with his military assignments. Pike was a high-ranking member of the Scottish Rite Freemasons, elected to the position of sovereign grand commander in 1859. He remained in this position until his death at the Scottish Rite Temple in DC in 1891. His legacy as a white supremacist persists today, and a statue of Pike in DC was forcibly torn down by demonstrators in 2020 following the death of George Floyd. Pike was laid to rest in Oak Hill Lot 541 East until 1944, when his remains were removed to be reburied inside of the Scottish Rite Masonic Lodge in the District of Columbia. (Left, courtesy of LOC; below, courtesy of LL.)

Maj. Gen. Edward Otho Cresap Ord was a Union general who commanded troops during the Battles of Dranesville and Vicksburg. Most notably, Ord was in charge of the troops that forced Gen. Robert E. Lee to surrender at Appamattox in 1865. While Ord was originally buried in Oak Hill following his death in 1881, the remains of the general and his wife were moved to Arlington National Cemetery in 1900. (Courtesy of LOC.)

Cadmus Marcellus Wilcox served with the US Army through the Mexican-American War, but the Southern captain resigned to join the Confederate army in 1861. Wilcox was made a general and participated in the Battle of Gettysburg in 1863 and the Siege of Petersburg in 1865. At his funeral in 1890, Wilcox was granted the high honor of being escorted to the grave by eight former Union and Confederate generals. (Courtesy of LOC.)

Col. John Harris spent 50 of the 70 years of his life in the service of the US Marine Corps. Harris enlisted in 1814 and participated in the end of the War of 1812, witnessing the battle at Fort McHenry in Baltimore. Harris was assigned command at sea until ordered to Florida to push out the native Seminole tribes in 1836. Harris intended to support American troops in Mexico, but an armistice had been reached upon his arrival. Harris was a well-respected leader and was appointed the sixth commandant of the Marine Corps in 1859. At the outbreak of the Civil War, almost half of the corps resigned to join the Confederacy, and Harris worked diligently to increase Union numbers. Harris is still honored by the Marine Corps, which leaves a wreath at his grave annually. (Left, courtesy of LOC; below, courtesy of LL.)

Rear Adm. Theodorus Bailey began his lifelong career with the US Navy at 12 years old as a midshipman in 1818. Bailey was promoted to lieutenant in 1827, and by the time the Mexican-American War began in 1846, he had already served tours sailing to the East and West Indies and Africa. At the outbreak of the Civil War, Bailey was ordered south, where in 1862 he notably walked through New Orleans to demand a Confederate surrender. Bailey was appointed to his final title of rear admiral in 1866 and retired the following year after 49 years of service to the US Navy. Bailey's monument in Oak Hill Lot 327 East includes a tribute to his naval service with a naval sloop carved above his name. (Right, courtesy of LOC; below, courtesy of LL.)

Rear Adm. Levin Mynn Powell served in the US Navy from 1813 to 1872, most notably during the second Seminole War in Florida. From 1836 to 1838, Powell was in command of the cutter *Washington*, and he engaged in the Battle of Loxahatchee. From 1838 to 1840, Powell's command was shifted to the USS *Consort*, followed by a post in the Washington DC Ordnance Office in 1848. During the Civil War, Powell sailed to the Gulf of Mexico on the USS *Potomac*, serving on blockade duty. He is interred in the Powell Mausoleum in Oak Hill Lot 291. The Powell Mausoleum was closed to the public following several incidents of vandalism in 1974. (Above, courtesy of LOC; below, courtesy of LL.)

Gen. George Douglas Ramsay entered West Point at 12 years old and graduated in 1820. On the eve of the Civil War, then-major Ramsay was appointed to a position on the Ordnance Board, and he quickly rose through the ranks to become chief of ordnance in 1863. Ramsay was made a major general in 1865 and commanded the Washington Arsenal until 1870. Ramsay rests in Oak Hill Lot 270 East. (Courtesy of LOC.)

Brig. Gen. Lorenzo Thomas graduated from West Point in 1823 and saw action during the Seminole, Mexican-American, and Civil Wars. Following Lincoln's assassination, new president Andrew Johnson attempted to appoint Thomas as his secretary of war, and it led to the president's impeachment in 1868. Thomas retired from military service on February 22, 1869, ten days before Johnson abandoned the presidency. Thomas is buried in Oak Hill Lot 259. (Courtesy of LOC.)

Rear Adm. William Branford Shubrick began his career in the US Navy as a midshipman in 1806 and spent 55 years in service, retiring in 1861. Shubrick was promoted to lieutenant on the eve of the start of the War of 1812 and was awarded a congressional medal for his capture of two British ships in 1813. Shubrick was overseeing the Bureau of Provisions and Clothing when the Mexican-American War broke in 1846, and he was assigned to sea duty. Shubrick ensured the safety of the Pacific theater while the war wrapped up. Despite his Southern heritage, he remained allegiant to the Union at the commencement of the Civil War. Shubrick was retired from naval service in 1862 and passed away in 1874. He is now buried in Lot 409. (Left, courtesy of LOC; below, courtesy of LL.)

Lt. Joseph Bryant Smith was the son of Rear Adm. Joseph Smith, a US Navy officer who had fought in the War of 1812 and the Mexican-American War. Undoubtedly influenced by his father, Smith enlisted with the US Navy in 1841 as a midshipman and graduated from the US Naval Academy in 1847. Smith was appointed a lieutenant in 1855 and served as first lieutenant of the frigate *Merrimack* from 1855 to 1857. Smith was then moved to the frigate *Congress* and was in command when it was attacked and destroyed by Confederate ironclad CSS *Virginia* on March 8, 1862. Upon hearing of the ship's surrender, Smith's father solemnly stated, "Then Joe is dead," knowing his son's strong patriotic convictions would result in death over surrender. The Smith family's cave-style mausoleum in Lot 215 is adorned with an ornamental anchor as a symbol of the Smith family's devotion to the US Navy. (Courtesy of LL.)

Gen. Charles Griffin (above) and Brig. Gen. Samuel Sprigg Carroll (right) were brothers by marriage who both served with the US Army during the Civil War. Griffin married Carroll's sister Sarah in 1861 after participating in the first Battle of Bull Run. Griffin was involved in further conflicts at the Battles of Antietam, the Wilderness, and Gettysburg before passing away in Texas from yellow fever in 1867. Samuel Sprigg Carroll also served with the Union army, leading troops through the Battles of Chancellorsville and Spotsylvania Court House. Carroll, having been injured on the battlefield, never fully recovered from his wounds and passed away in 1893. Both generals are interred inside the Carroll Mausoleum in Lot 292. (Both, courtesy of LOC.)

Gen. John Garland was an American soldier who spent 50 years of his life in service to the US Army. Garland joined up during the War of 1812, staying on with the Army in an administrative position at the close of the conflict. Garland was still following commands through the Seminole Wars and fought under future president Zachary Taylor at the front end of the Mexican-American War. Garland's actions were particularly distinguished during the Battles of Contreras and Churubusco, and he was promoted to brigadier general. Garland's daughter married future Confederate general James Longstreet in 1848, and the beginning of the Civil War brought tension between Garland and his son-in-law. He was still on active duty when he passed away in 1861. (Right, courtesy of LOC; below, courtesy of LL.)

Rear Adm. John Rodgers was an American naval officer who saw conflict through the Seminole and Civil Wars. Rodgers began his career as a midshipman in 1828 and spent a tour sailing through the Mediterranean Sea before the beginning of the Seminole Wars. In the 1850s, Rodgers took over the North Pacific Exploring and Surveying Expedition, and he was promoted to commander in 1855. During the Civil War, Rodgers made waves at Fort Sumter in South Carolina in 1863 when he captured the Confederate ship *Atlanta*. In the aftermath of the Civil War, Rodgers participated in a military expedition to Korea and returned to lead the US Naval Institute as president from 1879 to 1881. Rodgers passed away while working as the superintendent of the US Naval Observatory in 1882 and is buried in Oak Hill Lot 298. (Left, courtesy of LOC; below, courtesy of LL.)

Maxwell van Zandt Woodhull was born in Washington DC in 1843 and graduated from both the Miami University of Ohio and Columbian Law Schools before enlisting with the Union army in 1862. After four years of promotions, Woodhull was honored with the rank of brigadier general before mustering out of service in 1866. Woodhull practiced law following the war and is notable for his involvement with his alma mater, then known as the Columbian University in DC. He became a benefactor to the school and served as a trustee, convincing university officials to move the campus to the Foggy Bottom neighborhood of the city. The college became the George Washington University in 1904, and Woodhull donated his house to the university following his death in 1921. Woodhull is buried in Oak Hill Lot 580 East. (Above, courtesy of LOC; right, courtesy of LL.)

Georgetown was adjacent to the city of Washington DC until 1871 and acted as a separate city with its own jurisdiction. Henry Addison already owned a hardware business when he was elected to serve as Georgetown's mayor. He served three separate times from 1845 until he retired in 1867. Addison is buried with his family in Oak Hill Lot 18. (Courtesy of LL.)

Richard Wallach was an American politician who served as the mayor of Washington DC through the Civil War. While holding the title from 1861 to 1868, he helped establish DC's fire departments, paved roads throughout the city, and doubled the number of public schools within the city. Wallach is buried with his family in Oak Hill Lot 278. (Courtesy of LOC.)

David Yulee is remembered today as the first Jewish representative elected as a US senator, serving Florida from 1845 to 1851 and 1855 to 1861. Yulee owned a plantation in Florida, enslaved people, and further aligned himself with Confederate ideals in the years leading up to the Civil War. Yulee eventually harbored a fugitive Jefferson Davis in the fallout of the war and faced the longest prison sentence of any Confederate-affiliated civilian before being pardoned by Pres. Ulysses S. Grant. Yulee went on to rebuild the railroads of Florida and is also remembered as the "Father of Florida Railways." Yulee's marble monument in Oak Hill Lot 366 East is topped with an impressive angel, and the carvings upon it feature the writing of his wife, Nancy Christian Wickliffe Yulee. (Right, courtesy of LOC; below, courtesy of LL.)

Mary Elizabeth Thecker and Union army veteran Pvt. Robert Eugene Fugitt married on September 9, 1866, at Trinity Church in Georgetown. The couple purchased Oak Hill Lot 870 (pictured below) on August 14, 1869, and tragically buried their 11-month-old son 10 days later. Following the death of her husband in 1884, Mary was left a single mother, and she applied for a widow's pension, as was her right as a military spouse. Her son Robert E. Fugitt Jr. passed away in 1890. At the time this photograph was taken at C.M. Bell's photo studio in DC (between 1901 and 1903), Mary had been alone for more than 10 years. The button at her collar contains a photograph, most likely of her late husband. Mary joined her family at Oak Hill in 1914. (Left, courtesy of LOC; below, courtesy of LL.)

Three

LINCOLN CONNECTIONS

Abraham Lincoln is one of the most revered presidents in American history and has several connections to Oak Hill Cemetery. A few members of his presidential and cabinet staff rest here, and for a time, the connection was even more personal to the president. Lincoln's son Willie was temporarily buried in a mausoleum at Oak Hill, and visitors can still walk in the president's footsteps today. (Courtesy of OHC.)

Willie Lincoln (seated) was only nine years old when he passed away in the White House from typhoid fever in February 1862. Remembered as a precocious child, Willie loved to play and made friends easily. As the favorite child of the Lincolns, Willie's death forever changed the lives of his parents. Mary Todd Lincoln was so grief stricken that she did not attend Willie's funeral and never again entered the pair of rooms where Willie had died and been embalmed. After eulogizing his son in Oak Hill's chapel, a grieving President Lincoln returned to Oak Hill several times to visit his son's casket under the cover of night. Today, a donated plaque sitting inside of the Carroll Mausoleum continues to share the story of Willie's temporary interment. A fictional retelling of Willie's temporary interment at Oak Hill, *Lincoln in the Bardo*, was written by George Saunders in 2017, winning the Booker Prize and in turn cementing the Carroll Mausoleum as the most visited gravesite at Oak Hill Cemetery. (Courtesy of LOC.)

William Thomas Carroll was a clerk of the Supreme Court at the time Lincoln was elected and shared his family Bible for Lincoln to use for his inauguration. At the time of Willie's death, Carroll offered Lincoln a temporary place for Willie's body to rest as the Lincolns could not immediately return to their home in Illinois. The Carroll Mausoleum was complete and already held the remains of three other children when Willie was interred. Willie was removed from Oak Hill following Lincoln's assassination in 1865 and was reunited with his father for the funeral procession by train to Illinois. (Right, courtesy of LOC; below, courtesy of LL.)

John Nicolay, a German-born immigrant, served as the personal secretary for President Lincoln for the entirety of his presidency from 1861 to 1865. One of two personal secretaries, Nicolay (left), along with John Hay, worked closely with Lincoln in the White House. Following the death of Willie Lincoln, the president awoke a slumbering Nicolay to lament the loss of his son. Nicolay and Hay wrote a comprehensive and definitive biography of Lincoln following his assassination, and Nicolay spent time working in the US Consulate in France from 1865 to 1869. Nicolay was a founding member of the Literary Society of Washington, which his daughter Helen also joined. Nicolay and his family are buried beneath the memorial cube pictured below in Lot 273 East. (Left, courtesy of LOC; below, courtesy of LL.)

Jean Davenport was an accomplished English stage actress who found fame in Europe before traveling to the United States in 1838. By 1853, Davenport decided she was ready to move to America and began performing across the country. It was while she was touring in California that she met and married future Union general Frederick A. Lander in 1860. Davenport-Lander returned to Washington DC, and on the night of April 9, 1861, she overheard a group of men discussing a plot that would "change the world." Fearing for the life of President Lincoln, she immediately went to the White House to report what she heard to Lincoln's secretary John Hay. Following her husband's death in 1862, Davenport-Lander spent some time volunteering as an Army nurse before returning to the stage in 1865. She is buried in Lot 870. (Right, courtesy of LOC; below, courtesy of LL.)

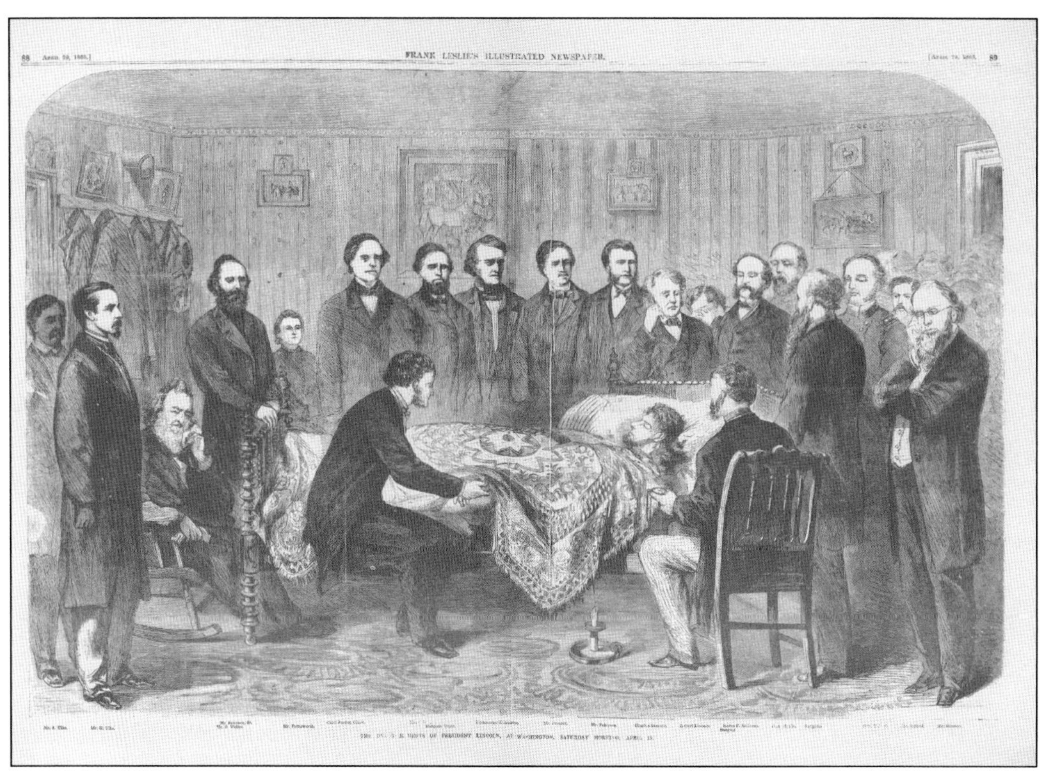

This etching of Lincoln's deathbed by Albert Berghaus displays a number of men who came into the Peterson House to assist President Lincoln as his life waned. Depicted in the foreground to the left is Henry Ulke, a resident at Peterson House. He boarded there with his brother, Julius, and the pair ran a photography studio around the corner on Pennsylvania Avenue. On the night of Lincoln's assassination, the Ulke brothers were eager to help the president and did so by running for supplies for the doctors caring for the president. Henry Ulke was also a talented painter and painted the (opposite page) portrait of Lincoln's secretary of war, Edwin McMasters Stanton, the man depicted opposite of Ulke in the above etching. (Above, courtesy of DCPL-PA; left, courtesy of SIA.)

Edwin Stanton was the first attorney to successfully argue a plea of insanity in 1859 for client Dan Sickles, setting an important precedent for the American legal system. In 1862, Stanton was appointed secretary of war by Abraham Lincoln and was tasked with organizing and supporting the mission of the Union army. On the night that Lincoln was shot at Ford's Theater, Stanton raced to the Peterson House and took charge of the investigation and manhunt for the team of culprits. Stanton kept his position as secretary of war for the beginning of President Johnson's term, and the attempt to replace Stanton led to Johnson's impeachment. Stanton passed away before he could accept President Grant's nomination to the Supreme Court and is buried in Oak Hill Lot 675. (Right, courtesy of SIA; below, courtesy of LL.)

After Lincoln was shot at Ford's Theater, Mary Todd Lincoln asked her son to send a carriage to Lafayette Square to gather friends Mary Cogswell Kinney, Mary's daughter Constance, and Mary's sister Elizabeth Dixon. In the parlor of the Peterson House, the ladies sat up through the night to comfort the first lady in her grief. Kinney's memorial stone at Oak Hill's Lot 931 is carved with her likeness. (Courtesy of LL.)

Brig. Gen. Joseph K. Barnes received his medical degree from the University of Pennsylvania in 1838 before he was mustered into the Union army and worked through the ranks to his position as the 12th surgeon general of the US Army. Following Lincoln's death at the Peterson House, General Barnes oversaw the president's autopsy. Barnes is buried in Oak Hill Lot 628. (Courtesy of LOC.)

Richard Merrick was an American lawyer who lived and worked in Georgetown from 1864. Merrick served as one of the defense lawyers for John Surratt, a Lincoln assassination coconspirator. One of Merrick's lasting legacies is an endowment at Georgetown University. The Merrick Medal is still awarded yearly to the best debater of the university's Philodemic Society. Merrick is buried in Oak Hill Lot 635. (Courtesy of LOC.)

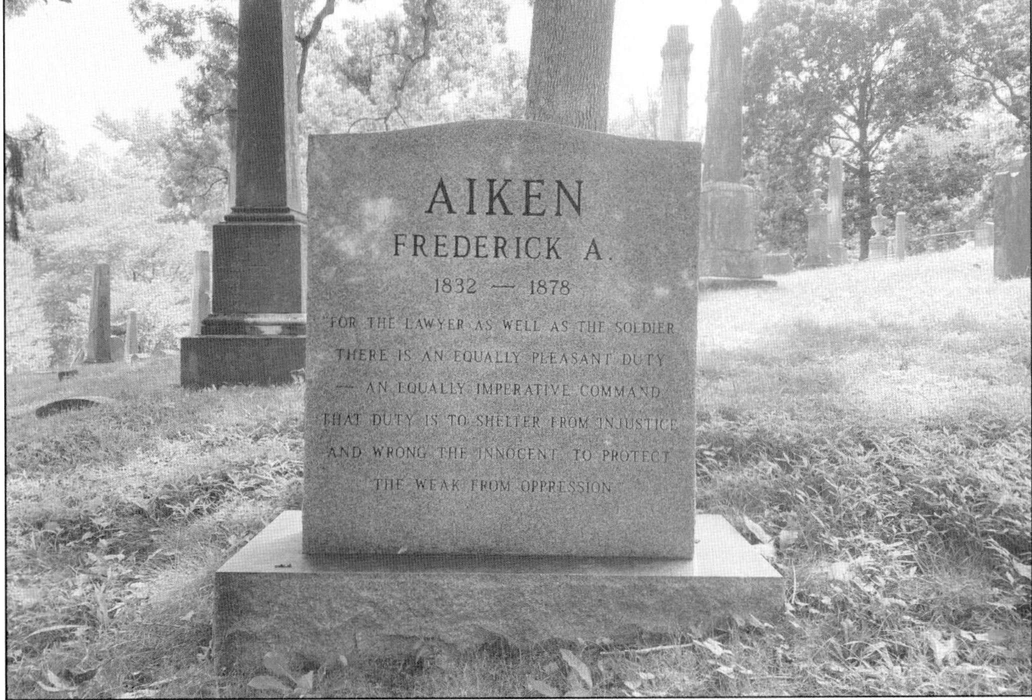

Frederick Aiken served as a court-appointed attorney for alleged Lincoln assassination coconspirator Mary Surratt. He worked diligently to save his client from the gallows, and the night before her execution, he went to the house of DC judge Andrew Wylie in a last-chance effort to save her life. Aiken did not have a headstone at Oak Hill until a generous donation from the Surratt Society in 2012. (Courtesy of LL.)

Andrew Wylie was a justice for the DC Supreme Court, and on the night before Mary Surratt's scheduled hanging, he wrote a writ of habeas corpus in a last-ditch effort to keep a lady from hanging. It was too late, unfortunately. The writ was not accepted, and Mary Surratt was the first woman executed by the US government. Wylie is buried in Oak Hill Lot 695. (Courtesy of LL.)

Noah Swayne was a lifelong Quaker and abolitionist who was so deeply disgusted by slavery that in 1826 he moved from Virginia to Ohio, where he began his own law practice. Swayne was appointed by President Lincoln to the position of associate justice of the Supreme Court and was sworn in as the 35th justice on January 27, 1862. Swayne is buried in Oak Hill Lot 179 East. (Courtesy of LOC.)

Four

POSTWAR RENAISSANCE

The end of the Civil War led to a period of growth and enlightenment within the federal city. No longer worried about war and conflict, DC continued to evolve into a city filled with art and culture, scientific and technological advancement, and stunning architecture. It was during this time that DC bloomed into the city it is today. (Courtesy of LOC.)

Joseph Henry was an American scientist who began his educational journey attending school at the Albany Academy in 1819, and by 1826, Henry had been named a professor of science at the same institution. While holding this teaching position, Henry experimented with magnets, discovering that tightly winding insulated wire around an iron core created a strong electromagnet. His invention of this powerful electromagnet led to an offer to teach at Princeton University, where he served as chair of the science department from 1832 to 1846. It was during Henry's tenure at Princeton that he was asked to become the first secretary of the new Smithsonian Institution in DC in 1846. While holding this position, Henry expanded the Smithsonian's mission to advance American science by supporting scientists at home and abroad and oversaw the publication of annual Smithsonian reports discussing a wide range of scientific studies like archaeology and biology. (Courtesy of LOC.)

As one of the perks of his position, Joseph Henry and his family were presented the exclusive opportunity to reside within the Smithsonian Institution's Castle following its construction. Henry, his wife Harriet, and their children Mary Anna, Helen Louise, Caroline, and William accepted the invitation to move from Princeton, New Jersey, to Washington DC in 1855. As the family made themselves at home in their apartment, Mary Henry was able to claim a room to use as a personal art studio. William Henry tragically passed away from typhoid fever in the family's Smithsonian apartment in 1862 and was buried in Princeton, New Jersey. Sixteen years later, in 1878, Joseph Henry passed away inside of the Smithsonian apartment. The Henry family was the only family ever permitted to reside within the Smithsonian Institution. (Both, courtesy of SIA.)

SMITHSONIAN INSTITUTION,

WASHINGTON, D. C., May 14 1878.

Dear Sir,

As Trustee & part owner of the Churchill vault, I have authorized the deposit in it of the remains of Prof. Joseph Henry until his family can obtain a lot in Oak Hill Cemetery to answer their purpose.

You will, therefore, make the necessary arrangements with Mr Buckley for the transfer to the vault after the services in the Chapel are completed, on Thursday next.

Respectfully Yours,

Spencer F. Baird

Superintendent of Oak Hill Cemetery
Georgetown
D.C.

At the time of Joseph Henry's death in 1878, no plans had been made for where he was to be buried. Henry's assistant secretary of 28 years at the Smithsonian, Spencer Fullerton Baird, offered the Henry family a temporary solution. In this letter from Oak Hill's archives, hand-written on Smithsonian Institution letterhead, Baird writes to Oak Hill's superintendent to grant permission for Henry's temporary interment in the Baird-Churchill Mausoleum. So it was written, so it was done, and it was there in Lot 279 that Joseph Henry rested from 1878 until 1880. During those two years, the Henry sisters and their mother worked together to make their own arrangements for a new family site within Oak Hill Cemetery called the Henry Crescent. The memorial on their site is comprised of a squat pink granite obelisk with matching footstones for each Henry interred there. (Courtesy of OHC.)

Spencer Fullerton Baird became the second secretary of the Smithsonian Institution in 1878 following the death of longtime boss Joseph Henry. Baird was an avid naturalist, and upon his appointment as the first curator of the Smithsonian Institution in 1850, he brought two boxcars full of biological specimens from his own personal collection to serve as the foundation for the institution's collections. In 1871, Pres. Ulysses S. Grant appointed Baird as the first director of the US Fish Commission, a title which he held until his death in 1887. Baird married wife Mary Helen Churchill in 1846, and the couple welcomed their daughter Lucy in 1848. The whole family is interred in the Baird-Churchill Mausoleum, found in Lot 279. (Both, courtesy of SIA.)

Baird (center) amassed a huge collection of natural specimens during his tenure at the Smithsonian and was tasked with building the Smithsonian's National Museum. Baird oversaw the construction of what is now called the Arts and Industries Building, which broke ground in 1879. The building was designed by German American architect Adolph Cluss, pictured third from the right. (Courtesy of SIA.)

Adolph Ludwig Cluss also designed Washington DC's Eastern Market and the Smithsonian's National Portrait Gallery, both of which still stand today. While Cluss denied any communist sympathies, he was nicknamed "The Red Architect" for the use of red brick in his work. He and his lovely wife Anita Cluss, pictured left, are buried together with their family in Oak Hill Lot 161 East. (Courtesy of LOC.)

In the same way that Spencer Fullerton Baird served as the longtime assistant of Joseph Henry, George Brown Goode spent the majority of his career as an assistant secretary to Spencer Fullerton Baird. Goode collected specimens for the Smithsonian Institution and assisted with Baird's fishery work from 1872 to 1888 and oversaw the daily operations of the Smithsonian's National Museum. The organizational systems used at the Smithsonian museums can be traced back to Goode. As noted on Goode's memorial stone, he designed the insignia for the Daughters of the American Revolution and served as a member of the organization's advisory committee. Goode and his family are buried in Oak Hill Lot 209 East. (Both, courtesy of LL.)

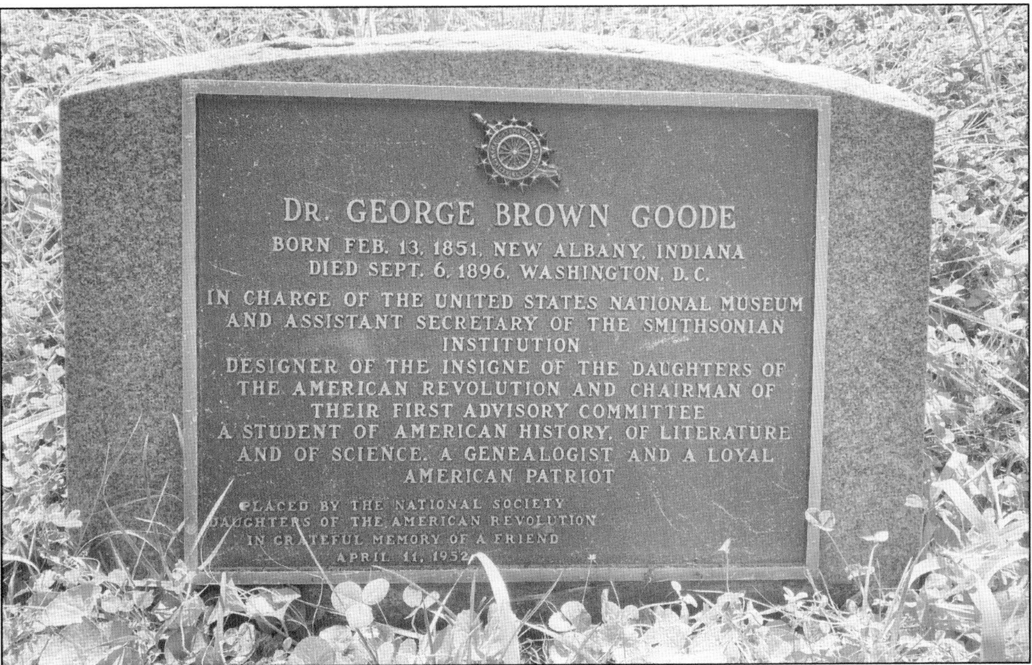

In the early days of the Smithsonian Institution, specimens collected by or donated to the institution were catalogued by a group of amateur scientists that referred to themselves as members of the "Megatherium Club." One of the members of this exclusive club, named after an extinct ancient sloth, was Henry Ulke, pictured on the top right of the club photograph. In addition to his successful career as a portrait painter, he collected over 125,000 beetles over his lifetime. He sold his trove to the Carnegie Museum of Natural History in 1902, and it is still considered a cornerstone of the Carnegie Museum's collections. The long-horned beetle pictured below, *Eburia ulkei*, is a part of Ulke's collection and is named in his honor. Henry Ulke passed away in 1910 and is buried in Oak Hill Lot 483 East. (Left, courtesy of SIA; below, courtesy of LL.)

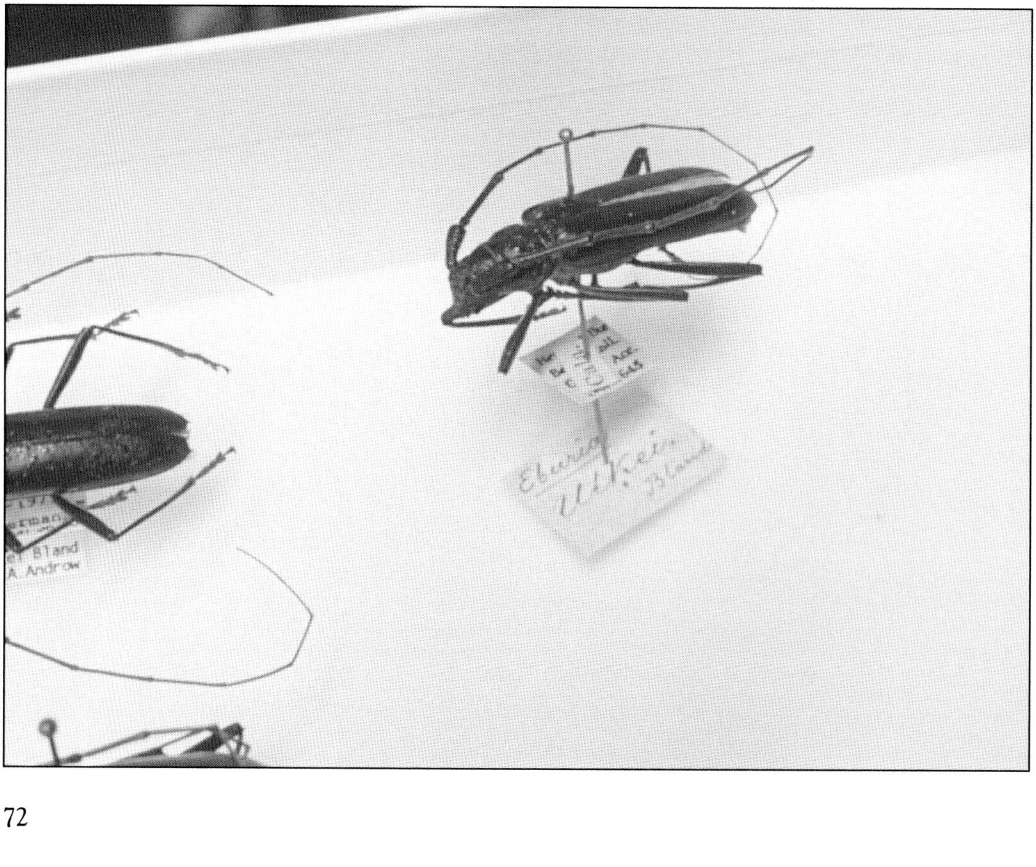

Dr. Theodore Gill was a rotating member of the Smithsonian's Megatherium Club and a biologist who was passionate about fish. Throughout his tenure with the Smithsonian Institution from 1867 to 1914, Gill cemented his reputation as a leading ichthyologist, with 388 of the 500 papers he wrote for the institution being written about fish. In addition to his work with the Smithsonian Institution, Gill spent time working as the assistant librarian of congress from 1866 and also taught zoology at the George Washington University. Gill was a founding member of DC's Cosmos Club, an invitation-only private social club that still exists today. Dr. Gill's descendant John W. Gill served as president of the Oak Hill Cemetery board of managers from 1972 to 2012. Dr. Theodore Gill is buried with his family in Oak Hill Lot 464 East. (Right, courtesy of SIA; below, courtesy of LL.)

Dr. Charles Rau was a Belgian archaeologist who immigrated to the United States in 1848 after receiving his education in Germany at the University of Heidelberg. Rau began his association with the Smithsonian Institution in 1863 by writing articles about his research into early American archaeology. Rau was a respected leader in his field and in 1875 was hired by the Smithsonian Institution as the first curator of antiquities for the National Museum. Rau received his doctorate from the German University of Freiburg in 1882 and continued to work with the Smithsonian until his death in 1887. Dr. Rau donated his personal collections and library to the National Museum, and he is buried in Oak Hill Border 4, Lot 59. (Left, courtesy of SIA; below, courtesy of LL.)

Julius Erasmus Hilgard immigrated to the United States at the age of 10 in 1835. In 1843, Hilgard traveled to Philadelphia to study engineering, which was the start of a long and successful career. He worked with the Smithsonian Institution in 1859 to create America's first self-recording magnetometer. Hilgard was recruited to the US Coastal Survey and was responsible for the charting and mapping of American coastlines through the time of his death. This work continued through the Civil War, as Hilgard offered his services to the US Navy and the Union army. In 1881 the US Coast Survey was renamed, and Hilgard served as the fifth superintendent of the US Coast and Geodetic Survey, until he resigned due to poor health in 1885. Hilgard is buried in Oak Hill Lot 714. (Right, courtesy of LOC; below courtesy of LL.)

Horace Capron was the oldest officer who served the Union during the Civil War, appointed as colonel of the 14th Illinois Cavalry in 1862 at the age of 58. Following an injury, Capron retired from service as a brigadier general in 1865 and was appointed as the commissioner of the US Department of Agriculture in 1867, which led to the government of Japan offering Capron $10,000 to transform the island of Hokkaido's agricultural landscape. Capron succeeded by introducing western cattle and seeds to the Japanese people, and Hokkaido evolved from scarcely inhabited to self-sufficient and prosperous. Capron was honored to meet Emperor Meiji three times before he returned to the United States in 1875. Capron's massive collection of Japanese art was sold to the Smithsonian following his burial in Oak Hill Lot 360 East in 1885. (Left, courtesy of LOC; below, courtesy of LL.)

Margaret "Peggy" O'Neill Eaton was born to a pair of hotel owners in Washington DC in 1799, and was raised working in the hotel bar. She married Tennessee senator John Eaton nine months after the death of her first husband. John Eaton was appointed to Pres. Andrew Jackson's cabinet as secretary of war, and Peggy was pulled from her life as a hard-working barmaid and raised to Washington's high society, much to the chagrin of the other cabinet wives. Thus began the infamous Petticoat Affair, in which President Jackson, in defense of Peggy, fired the members of his cabinet whose wives had been unwelcoming to her. She married a third time in 1859 to a dancing instructor who eventually ran away with her granddaughter and is buried in Lot 79. (Right, courtesy of LOC; below, courtesy of DCPL-PA.)

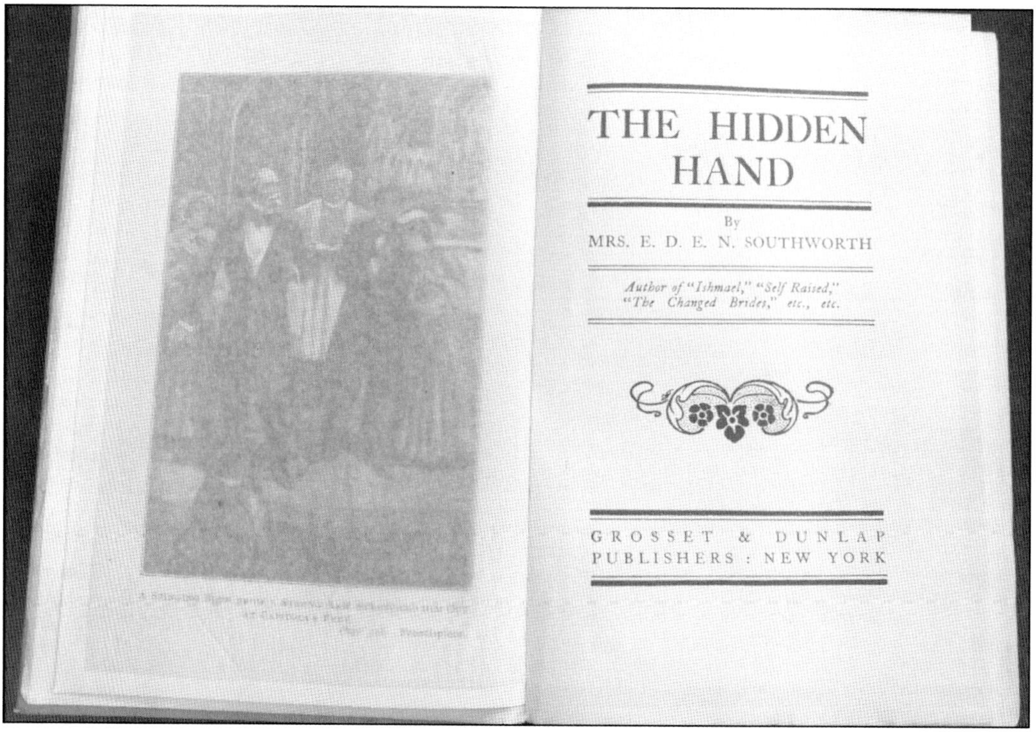

THE HIDDEN HAND

By

MRS. E. D. E. N. SOUTHWORTH

Author of "Ishmael," "Self Raised," "The Changed Brides," etc., etc.

GROSSET & DUNLAP
PUBLISHERS : NEW YORK

Emma Dorothy Eliza Nevitte, known by her married name of E.D.E.N. Southworth, was an American novelist who wrote more than 60 books during her lifetime. After her husband abandoned her and their two children, Southworth turned to writing to support her family, publishing her first story in a Baltimore newspaper in 1844. One publication led to more, and after several years of success in various newspapers, Southworth signed a valuable contract in 1857 to write for the *New York Ledger*, earning $10,000 a year for 30 years. With her hard-fought financial freedom won, Southworth purchased a house in Georgetown at the corner of Prospect Street and Thirty-Sixth Street overlooking the Potomac River. Her most famous novel, *The Hidden Hand*, is still taught in classic literature classes across the world. Southworth is buried in Oak Hill Lot 534. (Above, courtesy of OHC; below, courtesy of LL.)

Paul Pelz was a German American architect responsible for some of Washington DC's most impressive buildings. In 1873, Pelz was awarded the opportunity to building the Library of Congress's Thomas Jefferson Building, and the high quality of his work led to contracts all over DC and the United States. Here in Washington, Georgetown University's first major campus building, Healy Hall (above), was designed by Pelz and constructed between 1877 and 1879. Healy Hall is also home to another Pelz design: the Riggs Library (below), one of the only surviving cast-iron libraries of its kind. Pelz's other notable work includes the Keeper's House at Antietam National Cemetery in Maryland, as well Randall Hall and the University Hospital at the University of Virginia. Paul Pelz is buried with his second wife in Oak Hill Lot 992. (Both, courtesy of LOC.)

Herman Hollerith was a German American inventor and businessman who studied at the City College of New York and the Columbia School of Mines before joining the Massachusetts Institute of Technology as an instructor of mechanical engineering in 1882. By 1884, Hollerith had stopped teaching and began experimenting with a tabulating machine, using punch cards to record a desired data set. Hollerith's tabulating machine was used to record the 1890 US Census and completely changed the way census data was analyzed. Hollerith established the Tabulating Machine Company in 1896 and rented his equipment to countries all over the world for their own census work. In 1911, Hollerith sold his business to the Computing-Tabulating-Recording Company, which was renamed International Business Machines, or IBM, in 1924. Hollerith and his family now rest in Oak Hill Lot 654 East. (Left, courtesy of LOC; below, courtesy of LL.)

John Joyce was an American Civil War veteran and poet. Born in Kentucky, Joyce joined the 24th Kentucky Infantry Regiment in 1861 and, following success in the battles at Shiloh and Perryville, was promoted to the rank of first lieutenant. Following the war, Joyce spent some time working for the IRS and was eventually arrested as part of the Whiskey Ring. He was pardoned by President Hayes in 1877. Joyce was also a poet and is most famous for stealing the immortal lines "Laugh and the world laughs with you, weep and you weep alone" from lady poet Ella Wheeler Wilcox. Nevertheless, Joyce's memorial stone includes the stolen poem, as well as a crowd-funded bronze bust of his own face. He was buried in Oak Hill Lot 444 East. (Right, courtesy of LOC; below courtesy of LL.)

WASHINGTON, D. C.—FINAL INTERMENT OF THE REMAINS OF JOHN HOWARD PAYNE AT OAK HILL CEMETERY—THE MORTUARY SERVICES AT THE MONUMENT, JUNE 9TH.
FROM A SKETCH BY SPEDON AND A PHOTO. BY BELL.—SEE PAGE 287.

John Howard Payne was an American actor, composer, and diplomat, most famous in his day for writing the popular song "Home, Sweet Home." Payne's career began early as a child acting prodigy and evolved as he began composing music. In 1882, Payne found wide-reaching success with "Home, Sweet Home." Despite his fame, Payne struggled financially until he was appointed as an ambassador to Tunisia in 1842, and he passed away during his term abroad. W.W. Corcoran, founder of the cemetery and a lifetime fan of Payne, decided it was a travesty that Payne was not buried in his "home, sweet home" and paid to have Payne's remains brought back to Oak Hill Cemetery. On June 9, 1883, John Philip Sousa led the Marine Band in playing "Home, Sweet Home" during the grand re-interment ceremony, which was attended by Pres. Chester Arthur and the highest of Washington society. (Courtesy of OHC.)

Payne's striking bust was originally carved with a handsome beard until visitors spread a rumor that Payne had never worn facial hair during his life. The rumor came back to W.W. Corcoran, who had ordered the memorial stone, and he ordered that the beard be chiseled off. Payne was posthumously inducted into the Songwriters Hall of Fame in 1970. (Courtesy of LOC.)

Rev. William Pinkney was a bishop who served the Diocese of Maryland from 1870 to 1883 and was the religious officiant for the Payne re-interment on June 9, 1883. The Reverend Pinkney passed away just a few weeks after the Payne service and is buried just across from Payne on Oak Hill's Ellipse. (Courtesy of DCPL-PA.)

William Wilson Corcoran retired from his mercantile and banking businesses in 1854, turning his attention to philanthropic and personal projects. As founder of Oak Hill, Corcoran selected the finest sites at the cemetery for himself and commissioned Thomas U. Walker to build a Dorian temple-inspired mausoleum overlooking Rock Creek. (Courtesy of AAA.)

On the evening of January 31, 1892, five gunshots rang out on Q Street, fired by Howard J. Schneider. He had shot and killed his brother-in-law, 21-year-old Frank Hamlink, and mortally injured his wife, 23-year-old Amanda Hamlink Schneider, who passed away six days later. Schneider's trial was highly covered in the Washington press, and his victims are buried without a memorial stone in Lot 254. (Courtesy of LL.)

Amelia Heurich was the first wife of Washington DC's legendary brewmaster Christian Heurich. Amelia's marriage to Christian was a strategic decision for Heurich: Amelia was the widow of the man who owned the brewery before Heurich purchased it and thus was an indispensable resource and partner to the business. The couple was married for 11 years before Amelia passed from pneumonia in 1884. The Heurich House Museum in DC still displays a wreath preserved in paraffin wax from Amelia's funeral at Oak Hill Cemetery in 1884. Christian Heurich remarried twice more and buried the rest of his family at Rock Creek Cemetery in DC. Amelia forever rests in Oak Hill Lot 352 East. (Both, courtesy of LL.)

Ye Chun Ya was a member of the first Korean legation or diplomatic team to travel to the United States. Joined by his wife, Ye Chun Ya served as a secretary until he took over as an interim ambassador in 1888. The young couple, pictured to the left of the man in the top hat while visiting Mount Vernon, gave birth to a son in October 1890. Ye Washun, or "Son of Washington," was the first Korean to be born in America. Ye Washun tragically passed away at two months old and is buried in Oak Hill Lot 387 East, owned by the Phelps and Brown families, who originally rented and eventually sold their house to the Korean legation. (Above, courtesy of Mount Vernon Women's Association; below, courtesy of LL.)

Alice McClellan Birney was a mother and educator who was a cofounder of what would eventually become the Parent-Teacher Association. Alongside fellow cofounder Phoebe Livingston Hurst, Birney hosted the first meeting of the National Congress of Mothers in Washington DC in 1897 and served as president of the organization for five years. Birney is buried in Oak Hill Lot 67 East. (Courtesy of JCHS.)

Peter Parker served as a medical missionary to China from 1834 to 1855 and opened the Guangzhou Boji Hospital in Canton in 1835. Parker was forced to leave China in 1840 but returned two years later with his wife, who was the first western woman permitted to live in China. The Parkers returned to the United States in 1855 and are buried in Oak Hill Lot 511 East. (Courtesy of LL.)

James G. Blaine was a famed American politician who was most active in the years following the Civil War. Elected to the US House of Representatives for Maine in 1863, Blaine was further promoted to Speaker of the House, holding that positon from 1869 to 1875. As one of the most powerful men in Washington, Blaine transferred from the US House to the US Senate from 1876 until 1881. Blaine was then brought into the cabinet of Pres. James Garfield as secretary of state and was right next to the president when he was assassinated in September 1881. Blaine briefly held the same position in Chester Arthur's cabinet but resigned to pursue a presidential campaign. Blaine did become the Republican nominee but was not elected in 1884 and became secretary of state once again in 1889. (Courtesy of LOC.)

Blaine and his family moved into a stately mansion on Dupont Circle in 1882, and over the course of his work with the State Department, Blaine's son, Walker, was brought on as a solicitor. The two worked together closely in their respective offices until January 1892, when Walker Blaine fell ill after attending a party. Doctors were optimistic for Walker's recovery, but his health took a turn resulting in his death on January 15. The very next day, Blaine visited Oak Hill and purchased a burial site for his son in Lot 513 East. Just three weeks after Walker was interred, his sister Alice tragically passed away on February 2. Losing two children within a month forever changed the Blaine family, and the day after Alice's passing Blaine returned to Oak Hill to purchase the neighboring burial site for his own future use. James Blaine was buried at Oak Hill on January 30, 1893, in an elaborate funeral, pictured above. The remains of Blaine and his wife were taken back to Maine in 1920, but the Blaine children remain at Oak Hill. (Courtesy of OHC.)

Charles Milton Bell and his brothers are remembered in Washington DC for their family's photography studio, Bell & Brother (Bell & Bros.) on Pennsylvania Avenue, which was founded by Charles's brothers, Nephi, 19, and Thomas, 21 in 1862. Following the tragic deaths of Nephi in 1862 and Thomas in 1863, their father, Francis, and brother, Charles, took over the family business, securing deals with the government to photograph federal buildings and monuments in addition to their dealings with the families of Washington. Charles Milton and his wife are buried in Oak Hill Lot 626 East, which is just a stone's throw away from another Bell family plot in Lot 498, where Nephi Bell's photograph is embedded into the obelisk memorial stone. (Both, courtesy of LL.)

Five

A New Century

Washington DC greeted the 20th century with open arms, welcoming the bright minds of a new generation. It was during this time, with America expanding friendships abroad and the increase of federal appointments in the District, that a new generation of Washingtonians transformed the District from a stereotypical city into the diplomatic and governmental hub it is recognized as today. (Courtesy of LOC.)

Janet Bruce was born in England in 1848 and spent the majority of her youth in New Zealand. When she turned 16 years old, she began a career as an opera singer in Australia, adopting the stage name Jeannie Winston. Winston was active as an operatic soprano from 1861 through 1894, performing in light operas and often portraying masculine roles on stage. Winston toured the United States and eventually chose Washington DC as her home for the last 20 years of her life. In the summers, Winston continued to tour through Baltimore, DC, and Philadelphia until her passing in 1929. Jeannie Winston now rests in Lot Zero along Oak Hill's Border Two. (Left, courtesy of Huntington Library; below, courtesy of LL.)

Sophie Radford de Meissner was an educated American socialite who could speak English, French, and Russian. When her father was posted in charge of the US Navy in Europe from 1869 to 1870, she was given the chance to join him. Following their return to the United States, Sophie fell off of a horse in February 1877 and cracked her skull. She remained unconscious for almost a month, and while convalescing she welcomed many visitors, including Waldemar de Meissner, a secretary for the Russian Legation. The two fell in love and were married in November 1877. Sophie moved to Russia to join her son Sacha following her husband's death in 1896 and served as a lady-in-waiting to the Empress of Russia before returning to Washington DC in 1899. Sophie translated several plays from Russian to English before her death. (Right, courtesy of LOC; below, courtesy of LL.)

Albert Hulse Brooks is notable for serving as the chief geologist for the US Geological Survey of Alaska from 1903 to 1924. After graduating from Harvard University in 1894, Brooks continued his education abroad in Paris and Germany, returning to the States by 1898. Brooks participated in at least six expeditions into the Alaskan mountains for the Geological Survey and remained invested in Alaskan mineral industries until his death in 1924. Brooks was honored as the namesake of several sites in Alaska, including Brooks Falls and Brooks Lake in Katmai National Park and Preserve. The Brooks Mountain Range, stretching from arctic Alaska into the Canadian Yukon, was also named in his honor. Brooks now rests in Oak Hill Lot 339 East. (Left, courtesy of LOC; below, courtesy of LL.)

Frederic Wolter Huidekoper was a railroad baron from Pennsylvania who moved to Washington DC in 1883 and is notably honored with a city street being named after him. Found in the Glover Park neighborhood in Northwest DC, Huidekoper Place is located in one of the many neighborhoods that Huidekoper purchased and developed for residences in the District. Huidekoper is buried in Oak Hill Lot 971. (Courtesy of LL.)

Mary Virginia Merrick was the daughter of Georgetown lawyer Richard Merrick and the founder of the Christ Child Society. Paralyzed as a teenager, Merrick began to sew clothing for the poor children of Washington from her bed in honor of the Christ Child. Her organization has expanded since 1887 with 43 chapters across the Unites States. Merrick may achieve sainthood for her service to children. (Courtesy of LL.)

Alvey Augustus Adee began his career in foreign relations as the private secretary of Daniel Sickles in 1869, accompanying him to a post at the American Legation in Spain. Adee remained in Spain until 1877, when he returned to DC to work for the State Department. In 1886, Adee was appointed to the position of second assistant secretary of state, and he served in this capacity for 38 years. Adee was an avid biker and spent many summers biking across Europe in addition to biking to work daily. When Adee passed away in 1924, his funeral, pictured below, was attended by ambassadors from Germany, Japan, and Spain. Adee is buried in Oak Hill Lot 993. (Both, courtesy of LOC.)

Samuel Spencer was an American businessman and railroad president who tragically passed away in 1906 as the result of a train collision. The Spencer family plot at Oak Hill holds one of the cemetery's largest memorials, a striking angel that seems to emerge from the block of stone. This stunning funerary art was completed in 1907 by the artists at Tiffany Studios in New York. (Courtesy of LL.)

Edward Douglass White was an American lawyer who served as a senator from Louisiana before being appointed as an associate justice of the US Supreme Court in 1894. White was named the ninth chief justice of the Supreme Court in 1910 and held the position until his death in 1921. White is buried with his wife in Oak Hill Lot 600 East. (Courtesy of LL.)

William Tyler Page was an American civil servant and author who started working in the US House of Representatives at 13 years old in 1868. In 1919, Page was promoted to clerk, and he worked in this position until his retirement in 1931. Page was notable for winning a nationwide patriotic writing contest in 1918 that tasked entrants to describe the ideals of the American political culture. His "American Creed" has since been adopted into the naturalization process for new American citizens, and in 1955, the Daughters of the American Revolution erected a marble slab inscribed with Page's most famous work on his grave in Lot 635 East. (Left, courtesy of LOC; below, courtesy of LL.)

Dean Acheson was an American attorney who served as secretary of state under Pres. Harry Truman. After graduating from Harvard in 1915, Acheson married painter Alice Stanley in 1917. Acheson ventured into foreign affairs with the State Department in 1944, working in increasing capacities until his appointment to secretary of state by President Truman in 1949. Acheson was essential in the development of American foreign policy and was instrumental in the founding of the North Atlantic Treaty Organization (NATO) and the implementation of the Marshall Plan. Following his term, Acheson continued to work closely with the Oval Office as an advisor to presidents Johnson and Kennedy. Acheson was awarded the Presidential Medal of Freedom in 1964, and his memoirs of his time working in foreign policy won the Pulitzer Prize in 1970. Acheson and his family are buried in Chapel Lot 18. (Both, courtesy of LOC.)

David Kirkpatrick Este Bruce was an American lawyer and diplomat who spent the majority of his career working in international relations as an ambassador. Bruce represented the United States abroad in China, France, Germany, and the United Kingdom from 1949 through 1974 and served as the 10th US ambassador to NATO from 1974 until 1976. Bruce married his second wife, Evangeline, just three days after the divorce from his first wife was finalized, and the two raised several children together in Virginia. The couple are now buried next to each other in Oak Hill Chapel Lot 19. (Left, courtesy of LOC; below, courtesy of LL.)

Alvin Mason Lothrop was the cofounder of the popular Washington department store chain Woodward & Lothrop. Their large display windows facing potential customers on the street rivalled the splendor of Macy's windows, and customers flocked inside to purchase their fineries. After finding success with their first location in 1887, Woodward & Lothrop, known by locals as "Woodies," expanded into the DC suburbs of Maryland and Virginia. Woodward & Lothrop sadly declared bankruptcy following financial struggles in 1994 and is dearly missed by the Washingtonians that remember shopping there. The Lothrop family are buried in Oak Hill's Lot 428 East. (Above, courtesy of LL; below, courtesy of LOC.)

Joseph Edward Willard was the only child of former Confederate spy Antonia Ford and hotel cofounder Joseph C. Willard to reach adulthood. Willard spent eight years working in the Virginia House of Delegates and was elected as Virginia's lieutenant governor in 1902. Willard worked in this capacity for four years and notably was appointed as the American ambassador to Spain by Pres. Woodrow Wilson in 1913. The beautiful bronze artwork attached to Willard's grave is a copy of *Amor Caritas*, sculpted by Augustus St. Gaudens. The original once sat atop the memorial stone until it was stolen from the cemetery in the 1980s. Following the return of the stolen artwork, the original was replaced with the stunning copy found in Oak Hill Lot U East. (Left, courtesy of LOC; below, courtesy of LL.)

Six

Modern History

As time passes and the District of Columbia evolves, Oak Hill Cemetery remains unchanged in its mission to serve the Georgetown community. While many see this forest of memorials as a sign that Oak Hill is full, the beautiful garden cemetery continues to grow and bloom as staff work to create more burial sites for many future generations of Washingtonians. (Courtesy of LL.)

Armistead Peter III was a gifted artist and a Navy veteran, having served in both world wars. He married Caroline in 1920, and the couple were among the last of the Peter family members to reside in the historic Tudor Place. Following Caroline's death in 1965, Armistead created the Carostead Foundation with the intent to preserve the historic home. Tudor Place Historic House and Garden opened to the public as a museum on October 8, 1988, and interprets how the Peter families lived in the house over six generations. (Left, courtesy of Tudor Place Historic House and Garden, Washington DC; below, courtesy of LL.)

Stefan Osusky was born in 1889 in present-day Slovakia, which at the time belonged to the Austro-Hungarian Empire. Osusky grew up under imperial rule and expressed strong patriotic ideals against the empire from his youth. After receiving an education in the United States, Osusky went on to cofound the Czechoslovakian Republic in 1918 and also cofounded the League of Nations in 1920. He served as an ambassador for his country in England and France and fought against the rise of German Nazi culture in Czechoslovakia, continuing his work as minister of state while in exile and ultimately passed away in Herndon, Virginia, in 1973. (Right, courtesy of Willem van de Poll, Nationaal Archief/Van de Poll; below, courtesy of LL.)

Lawrence Quincy Mumford was the 11th librarian of congress from 1954 to 1974. The first trained librarian to hold the title, Quincy Mumford oversaw the acquisition and cataloging programs that doubled the library's holdings during his 20-year term. Mumford approved the construction of the James Madison Building for the library's campus in 1965 and helped secure necessary funding. Quincy Mumford is buried in Oak Hill Lot 650 East. (Courtesy of LL.)

David E. Finley was large in the DC art scene and served as the first director of the National Gallery of Art. Finley was also chairman of the US Commission of Fine Arts and a founding chairman for both the National Trust for Historic Preservation and the White House Historical Association. Finley was buried next to the Renwick Chapel at Oak Hill in 1977. (Courtesy of LL.)

Born in Philadelphia, Glenn Brenner (left) was a beloved American sports broadcaster who spent the majority of his career reporting for DC's WUSA 9 from 1977 to 1991. Known for his sense of humor, his segments like "Mystery Prognosticator," "Encore Wednesdays," and "Weenie of the Week" attracted many non-sports viewers to his fandom. Glenn had finished running his second Marine Corps Marathon in November 1991 when he suddenly passed out, and doctors worked for weeks before tragically discovering an inoperable brain tumor. Brenner fought bravely and passed away at the age of 44 in January 1992. Brenner is still remembered by longtime residents of the DC Metro area and is buried in Reno Hill Pathway Crypt Five. (Above, courtesy of Jerry Frishman; below, courtesy of LL.)

Katharine Graham became the first woman chief executive officer of a Fortune 500 company when she took the helm as publisher of the *Washington Post* newspaper in 1963. Graham paved the way for women in publishing and famously published the *Pentagon Papers*, containing details of the Vietnam War that many news sources were too scared to print. Graham lived right across the street from the cemetery, at 2920 R Street, NW. Graham was also known as a hostess and used her mansion on R Street to entertain countless politicians and notables, including John F. Kennedy and Jackie Kennedy Onassis. She is now buried next to Oak Hill's Renwick Chapel, almost in view of her longtime residence. (Left, courtesy of LOC; below, courtesy of LL.)

Ben Bradlee worked as the managing and executive editor of the *Washington Post* from 1965 to 1991. Over the course of his time at the *Post*, Bradlee is most known for his instrumental role alongside Katharine Graham in the publication of the *Pentagon Papers* and the Watergate scandal. Despite threats from the Justice Department, the pair authorized the Watergate story for print. Bradlee was a polarizing figure, and many criticized how his friendship with John F. Kennedy and other political celebrities in DC affected the articles published in the *Post*. Bradlee found love at the *Washington Post* in young reporter Sallie Quinn, and they wed in 1978. Following his retirement from his position as editor, Bradlee stayed involved with the *Washington Post*, holding the title of vice president at large until his passing in 2014. Bradlee's casket was held in a vault in the Renwick Chapel until his mausoleum was ready in 2016. (Courtesy of LL.)

Peggy Cooper Cafritz is best remembered as a cofounder of the Duke Ellington School for the Arts, which opened in 1974. She was also a collector of African American art and tragically lost a large portion of her collection to a house fire in 2009. Her memorial on Passionflower Pathway has a unique shape that could be described as a bean or a cloud. (Courtesy of LL.)

Vernon Jordan Jr. was a civil rights activist and lawyer who worked to desegregate the University of Georgia and spent time working with organizations such as the NAACP and the National Urban League. Jordan notably worked closely with Pres. Bill Clinton as an advisor in the 1990s and is buried in Oak Hill's Violet Pathway. (Courtesy of LOC.)

Chloethiel Woodard Smith was an American architect who taught architecture at the University of San Andres in Bolivia from 1942 to 1944 before returning to Washington DC and opening her own architecture firm. Nicknamed "Chloethiel's Corner," three of the four office buildings at the intersection of Connecticut Avenue and L Street were designed by her. (Courtesy of LOC.)

Arthur Cotton Moore was an architect who oversaw the renovations of many historic structures in Washington DC, including the Thomas Jefferson and John Adams Buildings of the Library of Congress and the Old Post Office Building. Moore's final project was his memorial on Oak Hill's Cross Avenue, called Arthur's Tree. (Courtesy of LL.)

Joseph Pozell, known as Joe, met future wife Ella on "The Hill" while they were both working in Congressional offices, and the two were happily wed in Washington DC on May 24, 1975. In 1986, Joe was appointed as the 10th superintendent of Oak Hill Cemetery, and the Pozell family moved into the cemetery's gatehouse. Joe and Ella dutifully served the Georgetown community together until 2005, when Joe was tragically killed while directing traffic at the intersection of M Street and Wisconsin Avenue in Georgetown. Ella Pozell took over as the 11th cemetery superintendent following Joe's passing and retired to North Carolina in 2012. Ella still returns to assist the cemetery office every year and will eventually join Joe in their site along Honeysuckle Pathway. (Left, courtesy of OHC; below, courtesy of LL.)

Madeleine Albright was a political scientist who served as an ambassador to the United Nations from 1993 to 1997 and notably served as the first woman secretary of state of the United States from 1997 to 2001. Born in Czechoslovakia, Albright and her family immigrated to the United States in 1948, and she became a US citizen 11 years later. After earning her doctorate from Columbia University in 1975, Albright worked with the National Security Council and later taught as a professor at Georgetown University before President Clinton appointed her to higher offices in the 1990s. Albright was also famous for her accessories: her brooches visually expressed her moods and opinions. Madeleine was the loving mother of three daughters and tackled single motherhood in addition to her world-changing work in international relations and policy. Following her funeral service at the National Cathedral in 2022, Albright was buried in a lot on the cemetery's North Hill. (Courtesy of LOC.)

In the 1980s and 1990s, cemetery board members faced a new challenge: creating new burial spaces within a historic cemetery. The Corcoran Plaza was constructed to combat this dilemma in 2017 and consists of a memorial wall with the names of the deceased carved into it, the sculpture *Diana's Lyre* by artist John Dreyfuss, and a dais with a door to deposit remains into a vault below. (Courtesy of LL.)

Completed in 2011, the Willow Columbarium is an open-air structure that contains 420 niches for cremated remains. All of the niches inside the columbarium are large enough for two urns, and niches can be combined to create a larger family-sized niche. The Willow Columbarium was designed by naval engineer Capt. David de Vicq, who has been a friend of the cemetery for more than 30 years. (Courtesy of LL.)

Seven

Cemetery Symbolism

The historic Oak Hill Cemetery is home to some of DC's oldest memorial stones and thousands of pieces of funerary art. Many of the images found on Victorian-era memorials are symbols that hold a deeper meaning and speak to the unending connection that humans share and cherish following a heavenly separation. (Courtesy of LOC.)

A memorial stone is the most common way to mark a grave and usually includes the full name as well as the dates of birth and death of the deceased. Memorial stones come in all shapes and sizes and can also feature funerary art and symbols, like the stone pictured above in Lot 687. Memorial stones placed for people who are not buried at the cemetery, like the one displayed below in Lot 397 East, are called cenotaphs. Of the over 19,700 burials at Oak Hill Cemetery, almost a third of the graves do not have a memorial stone at all and are currently listed as "unmarked." (Both, courtesy of LL.)

A headstone is a memorial stone that usually sits at the head of a gravesite and is the most common type of memorial at Oak Hill Cemetery. Headstones come in a wide variety of shapes and sizes and usually stand upright. In the same sense, footstone memorials can be found at the foot of the gravesite. They are generally much smaller stones set flush to the ground, only having room for one name or a set of initials, like the footstone pictured below in Lot 686. The photograph above, taken in Lot 514 East, feature both headstones and footstones for the two burials within. (Both, courtesy of LL.)

Urns are perhaps the oldest symbol of death, popularized in ancient Egypt and originally used to store the various remains of the pharaohs. At Oak Hill, urns can be found atop monuments large and small and often feature other symbols, like a drape or a wreath of flowers. The urn pictured at left is topped with an eternal flame, representing a legacy that will never die. (Courtesy of LL.)

Victorian funeral culture dictated the draping of black crepe cloth over mirrors so spirits would not get trapped in the earthly realm, symbolizing the veil between the living and the dead. Monuments at Oak Hill may feature drapes covering columns, urns, or the entire headstone, like this one in Lot 204. (Courtesy of LL.)

Obelisks are among Oak Hill Cemetery's most common symbols and can be found in almost every corner of the grounds. Obelisks became exceedingly popular in Washington DC during and following the construction of the Washington Monument on the National Mall from 1848 to 1888. An ancient Egyptian creation, obelisks symbolize a ray of sunshine shining up to light the soul's path to heaven. Obelisks can be made in any height and can be short and squat or tall and slender. Oak Hill's tallest obelisk belongs to the Orme family (pictured below) and can be found in Chapel Valley's Lot 774. (Both, courtesy of LL.)

Angels are known as heavenly hosts and messengers of God and are a common cemetery symbol across the world. Angels guard the gates of heaven in the same way they guard the souls of the deceased in a cemetery, ensuring the peace and safety of the departed. This angel, pictured in Lot 1011, was lovingly restored by cemetery staff following an act of vandalism. (Courtesy of LL.)

In the early days of the cemetery's history, popular fraternal organizations such as the Odd Fellows and the Freemasons performed secular funeral services for deceased members and would sometimes assist families in paying for funeral costs and memorial stones. Several stones in Oak Hill Cemetery bear the Odd Fellows insignia of three linked rings, including this one in Lot 354. (Courtesy of LL.)

While a monument in the style of a whole column stands as a symbol for a life fully lived, a monument that depicts a broken column symbolizes a life cut short or ended early. Oak Hill has many examples of this style at various heights, including this example in Lot 204. (Courtesy of LL.)

Following in the same vein as the broken column, a monument depicting a chopped or broken tree trunk symbolizes a life that was ended before it reached maturation or full bloom. This broken tree memorial in Lot 181 East is also covered in oak leaves and ivy, representing strength and immortality. (Courtesy of LL.)

A monument depicting a lamb represents an innocent life, typically decorating the graves of babies or young children. Many of the early sculpted marble lambs at Oak Hill, like these pictured in Lot 187, have eroded over the years and serve as a solemn reminder that even children can face death. (Courtesy of LL.)

There are no burials or headstones dedicated to pets at Oak Hill Cemetery, but visitors may find this friendly bronze dog pictured in Lot 173 ½ that watches over the grave of his beloved companion. Images of a dog in a cemetery can symbolize loyalty and devotion, always watching and protecting their loved ones where they lay. (Courtesy of LL.)

Flowers appear on memorials in every corner of Oak Hill Cemetery and have a long history with death and cemeteries. In the days before bodies were embalmed following death, flowers were brought in to cover the smell of the deceased. In a Victorian cemetery, flowers may be found carved in singular form or as part of a larger floral wreath, like the two shown here. Every flower has a different meaning, which makes floral bouquets a complex and multifaceted cemetery symbol. All flowers represent beauty, with lilies standing for purity and innocence, daisies for a childlike innocence, and roses for love. (Both, courtesy of LL.)

Ivy is a hardy evergreen plant that can be found in gardens and cemeteries alike, and since Oak Hill is a garden cemetery, it seems only fitting that keen eyes will find both carved and real ivy on the cemetery grounds. Ivy can be found on memorial stones all over the cemetery, including these two in Lot 518 East, representing immortality and friendship. (Courtesy of LL.)

While the majority of memorial stones carved to look like textured wood across America adorn the graves of former Woodsmen of America, Oak Hill's woody stones serve as a symbol of eternal strength and wisdom, harkening back to the biblical Tree of Knowledge. This stone monument was carved to resemble a tree trunk in Oak Hill Lot 553. (Courtesy of LL.)

Hands pointing either up or down were a popular funerary symbol during the Victorian era. A hand pointing up indicates that the departed soul is heading up towards heaven. Pictured in Lot 897, the upward-pointing hand above is also holding a sprig of lily of the valley flowers, symbolizing an innocent or pure soul ascending to heaven. Alternatively, a downward-facing hand, like this one in Lot 517, indicates a heavenly figure reaching down through the clouds to lead the virtuous departed soul upward to their heavenly rest, and raising the floral tributes left by their earthbound companions to the heavens as well. Keen cemetery visitors may also find hands stretching to the left or right, usually reaching for another hand on a neighboring stone. (Both, courtesy of LL.)

British artist Andy Goldsworthy created this beautiful granite stone bridge that now rests on Oak Hill's North Hill. Goldsworthy is known for making art from natural materials like leaves and dirt and creating immersive experiences in the wild outdoors. Goldsworthy's vision for this bridge monument did not stray far from the scope of his more popular work. The bridge was cut and carved from a single piece of granite and is meant to change over the coming years as nature grows and evolves around it, eventually staining the bright stone to a darker hue. Oak Hill Cemetery is now the only place in DC to see Goldsworthy's work outside of the National Gallery of Art. Designed for the Sant family and installed in 2022, this bridge is a functional piece of art that symbolizes the bridge between life and death. (Courtesy of LL.)

Bibliography

"Bodisco Memorial, Oak Hill, Washington, DC—1739." Postcard, 1928. The Willard R. Ross Postcard Collection, 1860–1948. DIG DC, The People's Archive, DC Public Library, Washington, DC.

"Chapel, Oak Hill Cemetery, Washington, DC—1798." The Willard R. Ross Postcard Collection, 1860–1948. DIG DC, The People's Archive, DC Public Library, Washington, DC.

"Jeannie Winston." Lithograph, c. 1887. The Jay T. Last Collection of Graphic Arts and Social History, Huntington Digital Library. The Huntington Library, San Marino, California.

"Eaton Memorial, Oak Hill, Washington, DC—1740." Postcard, 1928. The Willard R. Ross Postcard Collection, 1860–1948. DIG DC, The People's Archive, DC Public Library, Washington, DC.

"Pinkney Monument, Oak Hill, Washington, DC—1769." Postcard, 1928. The Willard R. Ross Postcard Collection, 1860–1948. DIG DC, The People's Archive, DC Public Library, Washington, DC.

Van de Poll, Willem. Portrait of Stefan Osusky. Negative, 1939. National Archives, The Hague, Netherlands.

"Van Ness Memorial, Oak Hill, Washington, DC—1768." Postcard, 1928. The Willard R. Ross Postcard Collection, 1860–1948. DIG DC, The People's Archive, DC Public Library, Washington, DC.

Discover Thousands of Local History Books Featuring Millions of Vintage Images

Arcadia Publishing, the leading local history publisher in the United States, is committed to making history accessible and meaningful through publishing books that celebrate and preserve the heritage of America's people and places.

Find more books like this at
www.arcadiapublishing.com

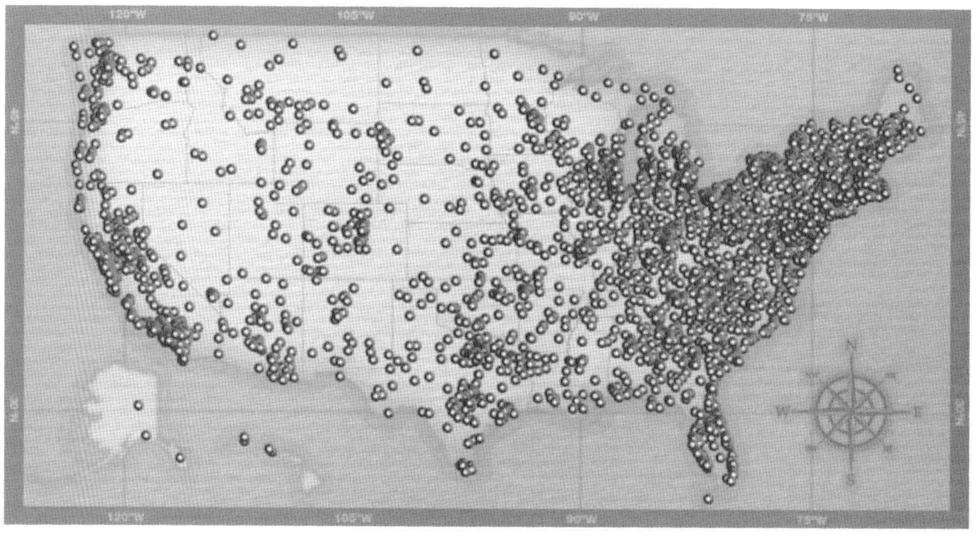

Search for your hometown history, your old stomping grounds, and even your favorite sports team.

Consistent with our mission to preserve history on a local level, this book was printed in South Carolina on American-made paper and manufactured entirely in the United States. Products carrying the accredited Forest Stewardship Council (FSC) label are printed on 100 percent FSC-certified paper.